New ENRICHMENT MATHEMATICS FOR PRIMARY

Pauline Ong
C. Ed. , B. Ed. , M. Ed.

 PAN PACIFIC PUBLICATIONS (S) PTE LTD

PAN PACIFIC PUBLICATIONS (S) PTE LTD
16 Fan Yoong Road Singapore 629793

First published 1996
Reprinted 1997
Reprinted 1999
Reprinted 2000

ISBN 981-208-374-X

Printed by C.O.S. Printers Pte Ltd.

PREFACE

New Enrichment Mathematics for Primary 1 – 6 is a series of six books specially written to help pupils with their revision. These books reinforce mathematical concepts learnt and help pupils to acquire skills necessary for problem solving.

The topical exercises and assessment papers included are consistent with those stipulated by the Ministry of Education in its latest syllabus. Each exercise is graded to cater to pupils with different abilities.

Pupils will find this series of books beneficial in helping them achieve better results in Mathematics.

Pauline Ong
C. Ed., B. Ed., M. Ed.

CONTENTS

4. Fill in the blanks with the missing numbers.

   (a) 4 138 means __4__ thousands, __1__ hundred,

       __3__ tens, __8__ ones.

   (b) 3 076 means __3__ thousands, __0__ hundreds,

       __7__ tens, __6__ ones.

   (c) 5 840 means __5__ thousands, __8__ hundreds,

       __4__ tens, __0__ ones.

   (d) 3 405 means __3__ thousands, __4__ hundreds,

       __0__ tens, __5__ ones.

   (e) 7 900 means __7__ thousands, __9__ hundreds,

       __0__ tens, __0__ ones.

5. Write the numbers.

   (a) | 5 hundreds 6 ones | 506

   (b) | 3 hundreds 8 tens | 380

   (c) | 9 hundreds 2 tens 7 ones | 927

   (d) | 3 thousands 4 tens 8 ones | 3048

   (e) | 5 thousands 9 hundreds 6 ones | 5906

6. Colour the spaces which contain the answer 1 000.

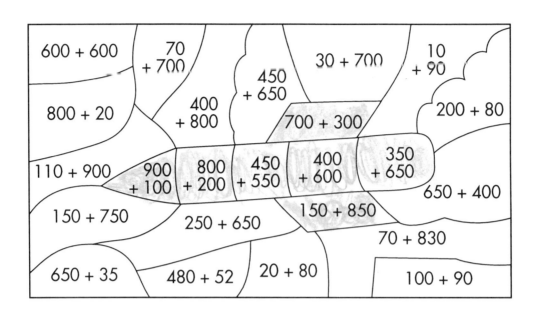

600 + 600	70 + 700
800 + 20	400 + 800

450 + 650

30 + 700   10 + 90

700 + 300   200 + 80

110 + 900   900 + 100   800 + 200   450 + 550   400 + 600   350 + 650

650 + 400

150 + 750   250 + 650   150 + 850

70 + 830

650 + 35   480 + 52   20 + 80   100 + 90

7. What does the digit 6 stand for in each of the following?

(a) 7 146   6 ones

(b) 9 654   600 hundreds

(c) 6 159   6000 thousands

(d) 8 563   60 tens

(e) 3 614   600 Hundreds

(f) 5 806   6 ones

8. Fill in the blanks with the correct answers.

(a) In 6 945, the digit __4__ is in the tens place.

(b) In 5 836, the digit __6__ is in the ones place.

(c) In 9 076, the digit __0__ is in the hundreds place.

(d) In 1 346, the digit __4__ is in the tens place.

(e) In 8 105, the digit __8__ is in the thousands place.

4

9. Complete these number patterns.

(a) 234, 235, 236, __237__, 238.

(b) 570, __580__, 590, __600__, 610.

(c) __1,450__, 1 500, 1 550, __1,600__, 1 650.

(d) 2 145, 3 145, __4,145__, __5,145__, 6 145.

(e) 2 600, 4 100, __5,600__, 7 100, __8,600__.

10. What is the whole number between ...

(a) 418 and 420? | 419 |

(b) 360 and 362? | 361 |

(c) 999 and 1 001? | 1,000 |

(d) 4 800 and 4 802? | 4,801 |

(e) 7 119 and 7 121? | 7,120 |

11. Fill in the missing numbers in the boxes.

(a) 10 less than 376 is | 366 |.

(b) | 1547 | is 1 000 more than 547.

(c) 7 540 is | 100 | less than 7 640.

(d) | 3056 | is 1 000 more than 2 056.

(e) 2 168 is 100 more than | 2068 |.

5

12. Write the missing numbers.

(a) 5 276 = 5 000 + [200] + 70 + 6

(b) 1 974 = 1 000 + 900 + 70 + [4]

(c) 6 048 = [6000] + 40 + 8

(d) 4 905 = 4 000 + [900] + 5

(e) 2 000 + 40 + 5 + 300 = [2345]

(f) 6 000 + 90 + 8 = [6098]

(g) 3 000 + 400 + 2 = [3402]

(h) 7 000 + 4 = [7004]

(i) 2 837 = [2000] + 800 + [30] + 7

(j) 9 099 = [9000] + [10] + 9

13. Write $>$, $<$, or $=$ in each $\bigcirc$.

(a) 905 $\bigcirc<$ 950

(b) 707 $\bigcirc<$ 717

(c) 818 $\bigcirc=$ 800 + 10 + 8

(d) 989 $\bigcirc>$ 1 000 − 21

(e) 4 104 $\bigcirc<$ 4 000 + 100 + 40

6

EXERCISE 2

—— *Addition And Subtraction* ——

1. Write the missing numbers.

(a) 46 + $\boxed{54}$ = 100

(b) 58 + $\boxed{42}$ = 100

(c) 135 + $\boxed{65}$ = 200

(d) 501 + $\boxed{299}$ = 800

(e) 766 + $\boxed{134}$ = 900

(f) 815 + $\boxed{185}$ = 1 000

(g) 745 + $\boxed{255}$ = 1 000

(h) 1 440 + $\boxed{560}$ = 2 000

(i) 2 382 + $\boxed{618}$ = 3 000

(j) 8 216 + $\boxed{784}$ = 9 000

7

William Truong #33
3-26-07

2. Do the following sums.

(a) $\quad$ 4 325 $+$ $\quad$ 5 473 $\quad$ 9 798	(b) $\quad$ 3 874 $+$ $\quad$ 125 $\quad$ 3 999	(c) $\quad$ 7 528 $+$ $\quad$ 849 $\quad$ 8 377
(d) $\quad$ 2 954 $+$ $\quad$ 1 046 $\quad$ 4 000	(e) $\quad$ 3 575 $+$ $\quad$ 438 $\quad$ 4 013	(f) $\quad$ 1 009 $+$ $\quad$ 998 $\quad$ 2 007
(g) $\quad$ 7 856 $-$ $\quad$ 4 735 $\quad$ 3 121	(h) $\quad$ 5 176 $-$ $\quad$ 487 $\quad$ 4 689	(i) $\quad$ 9 648 $-$ $\quad$ 825 $\quad$ 8 823
(j) $\quad$ 5 002 $-$ $\quad$ 3 153 $\quad$ 1 849	(k) $\quad$ 4 000 $-$ $\quad$ 897 $\quad$ 3 103	(l) $\quad$ 7 000 $-$ $\quad$ 4 852 $\quad$ 2 148
(m) $\quad$ 4 200 $-$ $\quad$ 695 $\quad$ 3 505	(n) $\quad$ 3 500 $-$ $\quad$ 1 750 $\quad$ 1 750	(o) $\quad$ 2 800 $-$ $\quad$ 1 975 $\quad$ 825

3. Write your answers in the boxes provided.

(a)	(b)	(c)
375 + **253** ———— 628	1 976 + **114** ———— 2 090	**711** + 576 ———— 1 287

(d)	(e)	(f)
569 + **335** ———— 904	**245** + 380 ———— 625	468 + **532** ———— 1 000

(g)	(h)	(i)
576 − **289** ———— 287	4 520 − **1 870** ———— 2 650	5 000 − **2 500** ———— 2 500

4. Complete the following.

(a) $137 + 3 =$ **140**

(b) $576 + 14 =$ **590**

(c) $1\ 576 -$ **1079** $= 497$

(d) **2930** $- 385 = 2\ 545$

(e) $2\ 100 -$ **1950** $= 150$

(f) 5 000 – 2 575 = ⬛ 2425

(g) 2 000 – ⬛ 200 = 1 800

(h) ⬛ 3750 + 1 250 = 5 000

(i) 8 100 + ⬛ 900 = 9 000

(j) 1 080 – ⬛ 820 = 260

(k) 1 473 + ⬛ 1527 = 3 000

(l) 1 234 + ⬛ 3097 = 4 321

Do these sums carefully showing all your working and statements.

5. Derong had 473 stamps.
    His brother had 523 stamps more than him.
    How many stamps did they have altogether?

$$
\begin{array}{r}
^14\,7\,3 \\
+\,5\,2\,3 \\
\hline
1\,0\,3\,6
\end{array}
$$

They had ___1036___ stamps altogether.

6. After giving 145 marbles to his friends, Ali had 755 marbles left. How many marbles did Ali have at first?

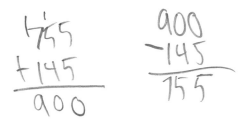

Ali had ___900___ marbles at first.

7. A computer costs $3 250.
   It costs $1 080 more than a television set.
   How much does the television set cost?

The television set costs ___$2170___.

8. Meiling collected 1 680 seashells.
   She collected 795 more seashells than Sumei.
   How many seashells did Sumei collect?

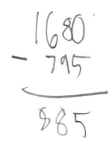

Sumei collected ___885___ seashells.

11

9. Mr Tan sold 560 mangoes on Saturday.
   He sold 340 more mangoes on Sunday than on Saturday.
   How many mangoes were sold on both days?

   _____900_____ mangoes were sold on both days.

10. At an exhibition, there were 1 450 men and 740 women.
    There were 600 fewer children than adults.
    How many people were there at the exhibition?

    There were _____1590_____ people at the exhibition.

REVISION 1

Name: William Truong

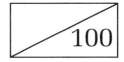

Marks: /100

Date: 4-1-07

Time allowed: 1 h 30 min

Section A (20 × 2 marks)

Choose the correct answer and write its number in the brackets provided.

1. Which of the following gives 97?
    (1) 67 + 20   (2) 64 + 8
    (3) 72 + 5   (4) 60 + 37   (4)

2. Which of the following numbers is 70 more than 350?
    (1) 280   (2) 290
    (3) 320   (4) 420   (4)

3. 3 802 is the same as _____.
    (1) three hundred and eighty-two
    (2) three thousand, eight hundred and two
    (3) three thousand, eight hundred and twenty
    (4) three thousand and eighty-two   (2)

4. 5 000 + 300 + 6 = ☐.
    The missing number in the box is 5 306.
    (1) 5 036   (2) 5 306
    (3) 5 360   (4) 5 603   (2)

5. Which one of the numbers has the digit 4 in the hundreds place?
    (1) 2 346   (2) 4 765
    (3) 8 431   (4) 9 654   (3)

6. What is the next number in the number pattern below?

65, 71, 77, __83__.

(1) 79   (2) 80

(3) 83   (4) 85   (3)

7. 4 444 is the same as __4 440 + 4__.

(1) 444 + 4   (2) 4 044 + 4

(3) 4 404 + 4   (4) 4 440 + 4   (4)

8. The sum of 27 and 215 is __242__.

(1) 242   (2) 342

(3) 485   (4) 540   (1)

9. If 27 is taken away from 45, the answer is __18__.

(1) 17   (2) 18

(3) 19   (4) 72   (2)

10. The number that is 1 less than 4 328 is __4327__.

(1) 4 228   (2) 4 318

(3) 4 327   (4) 4 329   (3)

11. If 526 is added to 1 294, the answer will be __1820__.

(1) 768   (2) 1 802

(3) 1 820   (4) 6 554   (3)

12. 376 + [458] = 834.

The missing number in the box is __458__.

(1) 454   (2) 458

(3) 464   (4) 1 210   (2)

13. In 4 000 + [800] + 70 + 6 = 4 876, the missing number in the box is __800__.

(1) 8   (2) 80

(3) 800   (4) 8 000   (3)

14. Which of these numbers is the smallest?
    (1) 4 490   (2) 4 904
    (3) 4 940   (4) 4 049   (4)

15. Which number is less than 705 by 50?
    (1) 205   (2) 655
    (3) 700   (4) 755   (2)

16. Which number is 1 less than 1 000?
    (1) 100   (2) 990
    (3) 999   (4) 9 099   (3)

17. The largest 4-digit number that can be formed from the digits shown
    below is _6410_.

                        0, 4, 6, 1

    (1) 1 046   (2) 6 410
    (3) 6 401   (4) 1 460   (2)

18. 5 thousands, 7 hundreds and 3 ones is the same as _5703_.
    (1) 5 703   (2) 5 730
    (3) 5 073   (4) 5 037   (1)

19. [7701] is 1 000 more than 6 701.
    (1) 7 701   (2) 6 801
    (3) 6 710   (4) 5 701   (1)

20. Ali has 1 086 stamps.
    Ahmad has 854 stamps.
    Ali has _232_ stamps more than Ahmad.
    (1) 232   (2) 322
    (3) 1 940   (4) 9 676   (1)

15

Section B (20 × 2 marks)

Write your answers in the boxes provided.

21. 2 000 + 5 + 30 = 2035 .

22. What is the missing number in the number pattern below?

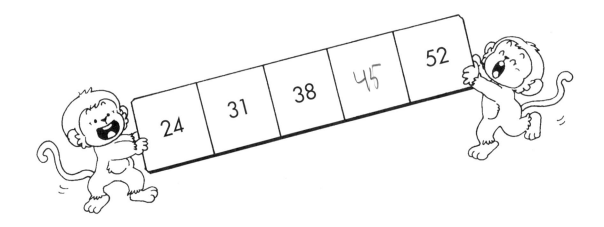

24   31   38   45   52

23. Nine thousand, three hundred and four written as a numeral is
    9,304 .

24. 4 thousands + 24 hundreds = 6400

25. 728 + 272 = 1 000

26. 1 448 − 768 = 680

27. 10 000 = 100 hundreds

28. Arrange these numbers in order, beginning with the smallest.
    1 022, 1 202, 1 002, 1 220.

    1002, 1022, 1220, 1202

16

29. In 7 450, which digit is in the hundreds place? `4`

30. What does the digit 8 in 8 145 stand for? `8000 thousands`

31. `4285` − 1 285 = 3 000

32. 125 + `550` + 325 = 1 000

33. There are 1 796 pupils in a school.
    897 of them are boys. How many girls are there? `899`

34. Put >, <, or = in the box.

    10 000 − 3 000 `>` 6 999

35. 5 000 − `3500` = 1 500

36. After spending $448 on a video cassette recorder, Mr Lin had $552
    left. How much money had he at first? `$970.00`

37. There are 1 096 girls and 1 275 boys in a school.
    How many children are there in the school? `2371`

38. Lisa had 1 456 buttons. She had 259 more buttons than Tina.
    How many buttons had Tina? `1197`

17

39. 1 346 pupils went to the Science Centre on Tuesday and 2 967 pupils went on Wednesday. How many pupils visited the Science Centre during the two days?

4313

40. A fast food restaurant sold 5 060 hamburgers on Saturday and Sunday. 2 789 hamburgers were sold on Saturday. How many hamburgers were sold on Sunday?

2271

Section C (5 × 4 marks)

Work out the following sums in the space provided. Show all your working and steps clearly.

41. Mr Chen bought 1 248 bulbs for decorations.
He found that 19 bulbs were defective.
How many bulbs were not defective?

$$\begin{array}{r} 1\overset{3}{2}\overset{18}{4}\overset{}{8} \\ -\quad 19 \\ \hline 1229 \end{array}$$

Answer: 1229

42. Madam Cheng has 1 704 green beads.
There are 690 fewer green beads than red ones.
How many red beads are there?

$$1704$$
$$-\ 690$$
$$\overline{1014}$$

Answer: 1014

43. A stamp album can hold 800 stamps.
Lina has 488 stamps.
How many more stamps does she need to fill the album?

$$800$$
$$+\ 488$$
$$\overline{312}$$

Answer: 312

44. Mr Ahmad and Mr Ng caught 1 200 fish altogether.
Mr Ahmad caught 580 fish.
Mr Ng lost 85 fish when his net tore.
How many fish had Mr Ng left?

$$1200$$
$$-\ 580$$
$$\overline{620}$$

$$620$$
$$-\ 85$$
$$\overline{535}$$

Answer: 535

45. Cinema A can hold 850 people.
   Cinema B can hold 250 more people than Cinema A.
   Cinema C can hold 350 less people than the total number of people
   held by Cinema A and Cinema B.
   How many seats can Cinema C hold?

$$\begin{array}{r} 850 \\ + 250 \\ \hline 1100 \end{array} \qquad \begin{array}{r} 1100 \\ - 350 \\ \hline 750 \end{array}$$

Answer: 750

Multiplication And Division

1. Complete these number patterns.

   (a) 3, | 6 |, 9, | 12 |, 15

   (b) 4, 8, | 12 |, 16, | 20 |

   (c) 7, 14, | 21 |, | 28 |, 35

   (d) 24, 30, | 36 |, 42, | 48 |, 54

   (e) | 37 |, 45, | 53 |, 63, 72

2. Fill in the boxes with the correct answers.

   (a) 6 × | 3 | = 18   (b) 3 × | 8 | = 24

   (c) 10 × 5 = | 50 | (d) 0 × 4 = | 0 |

   (e) 20 ÷ | 4 | = 5   (f) | 40 | ÷ 10 = 4

   (g) 70 ÷ | 10 | = 7   (h) | 0 | ÷ 2 = 0

   (i) | 9 | × 4 = 40 − 4   (j) 40 ÷ | 4 | = 20 ÷ 2

   (k) 8 × | 2 | = 8 + 8   (l) | 27 | ÷ 3 = 36 ÷ 4

   (m) | 10 | × 4 = 5 × 4 + 4

   (n) 7 × 4 = 7 × 3 + | 7 |

21

3. Fill in the ◯ with ÷ or ×.

(a) 8 ⊗ 5 = 40

(b) 32 ⊕ 4 = 8

(c) 9 ⊗ 4 = 36

(d) 16 ÷ 4 = 4

(e) 12 ÷ 3 = 4

(f) 7 ⊗ 3 = 21

(g) 20 ÷ 2 = 10

(h) 5 ⊗ 7 = 35

(i) 14 ÷ 7 = 2

(j) 11 ⊗ 5 = 55

4. Match.

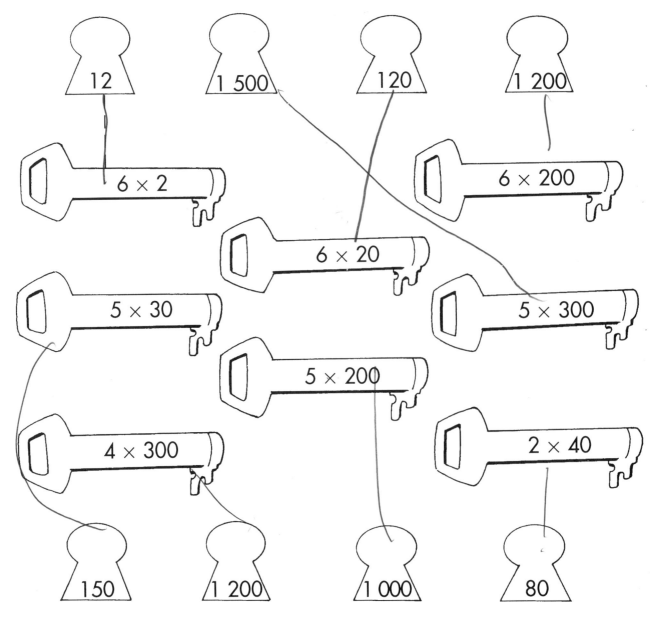

5. Find the product for each of the following.

    (a) $18 \times 3 =$ __54__

    (b) $59 \times 4 =$ __236__

    (c) $5 \times 40 =$ __200__

    (d) $10 \times 60 =$ __600__

    (e) $274 \times 2 =$ __548__

    (f) $855 \times 3 =$ __2565__

    (g) $700 \times 10 =$ __7000__

    (h) $186 \times 4 =$ __744__

    (i) $4 \times 504 =$ __2016__

    (j) $5 \times 327 =$ __1635__

6. Find the quotient and remainder.

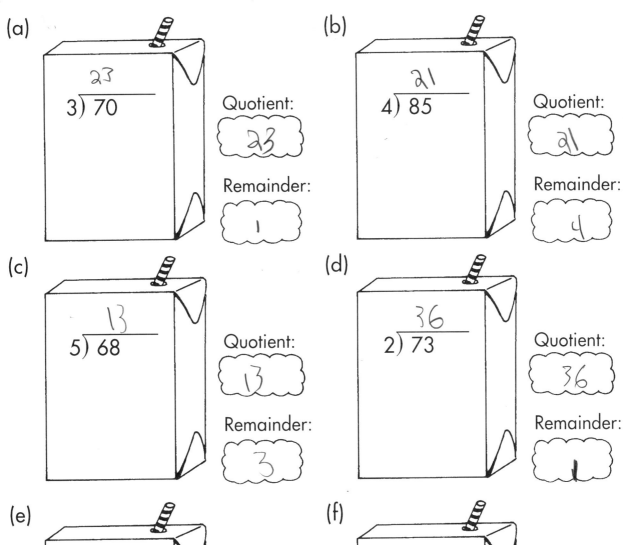

(a)
$$3\overline{)\,70}$$ 23

Quotient: 23

Remainder: 1

(b)
$$4\overline{)\,85}$$ 21

Quotient: 21

Remainder: 4

(c)
$$5\overline{)\,68}$$ 13

Quotient: 13

Remainder: 3

(d)
$$2\overline{)\,73}$$ 36

Quotient: 36

Remainder: 1

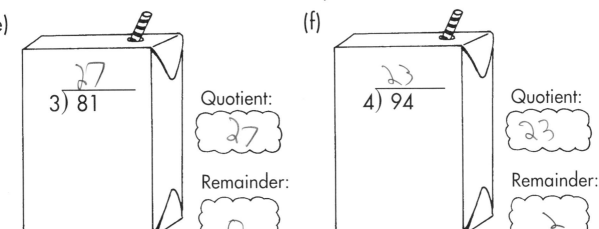

(e)
$$3\overline{)\,81}$$ 27

Quotient: 27

Remainder: 0

(f)
$$4\overline{)\,94}$$ 23

Quotient: 23

Remainder: 2

23

7. Match the cups and saucers.

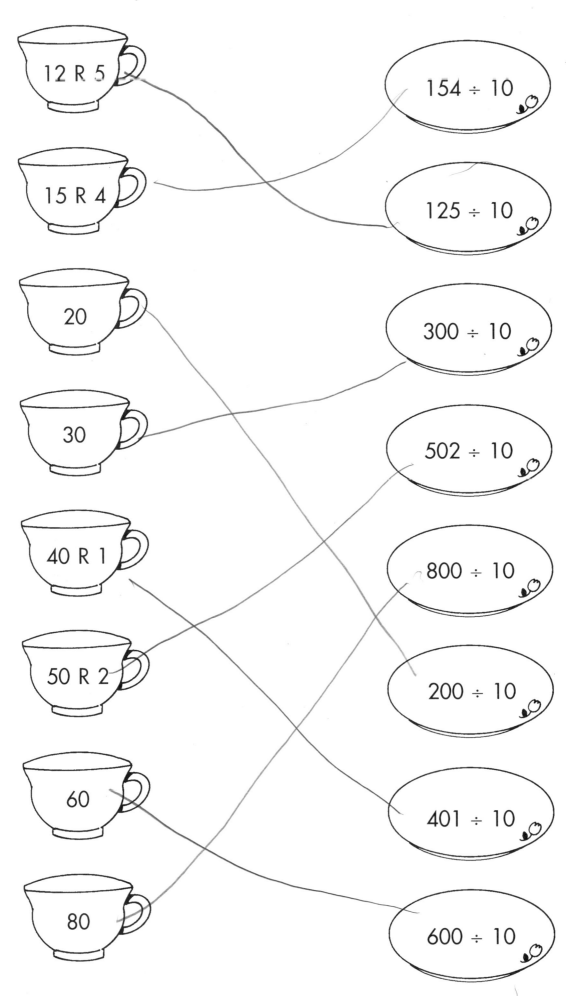

12 R 5

15 R 4

20

30

40 R 1

50 R 2

60

80

154 ÷ 10

125 ÷ 10

300 ÷ 10

502 ÷ 10

800 ÷ 10

200 ÷ 10

401 ÷ 10

600 ÷ 10

Work out the following sums in the space provided. Show all your working and steps clearly.

8. Rina has 3 times as many stickers as Siti.
   If Siti has 9 stickers, how many stickers does Rina have?

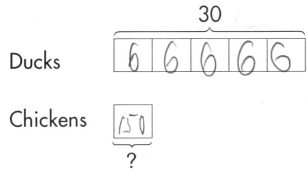

Rina | 3 | 3 | 3 |
︸
?

Siti | 3 |
︸
9

Answer: | 27 |

9. There are 30 ducks on Mr Mac's farm.
   There are 5 times as many ducks as chickens.
   How many chickens are there?

   30
   ⏞
   Ducks | 6 | 6 | 6 | 6 | 6 |

   Chickens | 150 |
   ︸
   ?

   Answer: | 150 |

10. There are 42 chairs in a classroom.
    How many chairs are there in 8 similar classrooms?

    Answer: | 336 |

11. Ravi saved $90 for 5 months.
    If he saved the same amount for each month, how much did he save in one month?

$$5 \overline{)90} \quad \frac{18}{}$$

Answer: 18

12. Meiling puts 96 exercise books equally into 6 piles.
    How many exercise books are there in one pile?

Answer: 16

13. A chicken egg costs 12 cents.
    A duck egg costs 3 cents more than a chicken egg.
    How much will Mrs Lin have to pay the egg seller if she buys 10 chicken eggs and 5 duck eggs?

Answer: 75

14. Baoling had 175 stamps.
    She put 10 stamps on each page of an album.
    How many pages did she use?

Answer: 17 5 remainder

15. 6 boys and 4 girls shared the cost of a present equally.
    If each of them paid $14, how much did the present cost?

Answer: 336

—Multiplication Tables Of 6, 7, 8 And 9—

6 - 2 - 07

1. Complete the number sentences.

(a) $\boxed{6} \times 2 = 12$

(b) $\boxed{7} \times 3 = 21$

$12 \div 2 = \boxed{6}$

$21 \div 3 = \boxed{7}$

(c) $\boxed{8} \times 2 = 16$

(d) $\boxed{9} \times 4 = 36$

$16 \div 2 = \boxed{8}$

$36 \div 4 = \boxed{9}$

(e) $4 \times \boxed{6} = 24$

(f) $5 \times \boxed{7} = 35$

$24 \div 4 = \boxed{6}$

$35 \div 5 = \boxed{7}$

(g) 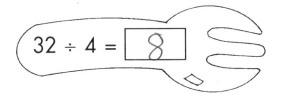 $4 \times \boxed{8} = 32$

(h) $6 \times \boxed{9} = 54$

$32 \div 4 = \boxed{8}$

$54 \div 6 = \boxed{9}$

(i) $8 \times \boxed{6} = 48$

(j) $2 \times \boxed{9} = 18$

$48 \div 8 = \boxed{6}$

$18 \div 2 = \boxed{9}$

2. Multiply.

(a) $\begin{array}{r} ^3 16 \\ \times\ \ 6 \\ \hline 96 \end{array}$	(b) $\begin{array}{r} ^4 17 \\ \times\ \ 7 \\ \hline 119 \end{array}$	(c) $\begin{array}{r} 21 \\ \times\ \ 8 \\ \hline 168 \end{array}$
(d) $\begin{array}{r} ^1 12 \\ \times\ \ 9 \\ \hline 108 \end{array}$	(e) $\begin{array}{r} ^3 45 \\ \times\ \ 6 \\ \hline 270 \end{array}$	(f) $\begin{array}{r} ^1 62 \\ \times\ \ 9 \\ \hline 558 \end{array}$
(g) $\begin{array}{r} ^1 32 \\ \times\ \ 7 \\ \hline 224 \end{array}$	(h) $\begin{array}{r} ^3 54 \\ \times\ \ 8 \\ \hline 432 \end{array}$	(i) $\begin{array}{r} ^7 78 \\ \times\ \ 9 \\ \hline 702 \end{array}$

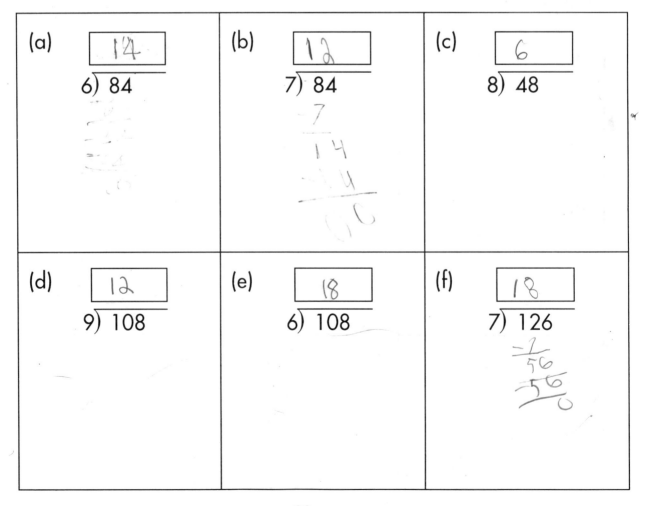

(j) ¹120 × 6 = 720	(k) 212 × 7 = 1,484	(l) ²⁶328 × 8 = 2,624
(m) ¹³414 × 9 = 3,726	(n) ¹²123 × 8 = 984	(o) 501 × 6 = 3006
(p) ²613 × 7 = 4291	(q) ¹721 × 8 = 5768	(r) 901 × 6 = 5406

3. Divide.

(a) 14
6) 84

(b) 12
7) 84
  7
  14
  14
  0

(c) 6
8) 48

(d) 12
9) 108

(e) 18
6) 108

(f) 18
7) 126
  7
  56
  56
  0

(g)

$\boxed{14}$

$8)\overline{112}$

(h)

$\boxed{20}$

$7)\overline{140}$

(i)

$\boxed{13}$

$9)\overline{117}$

(j)

$\boxed{17}$

$6)\overline{102}$

(k)

$\boxed{61}$

$7)\overline{427}$

(l)

$\boxed{24}$

$9)\overline{216}$

(m)

$\boxed{8}\,)\,\dfrac{101}{808}$

(n)

$\boxed{9}\,)\,\dfrac{34}{306}$

(o)

$\boxed{7}\,)\,\dfrac{73}{511}$

(p)

$\boxed{6}\,)\,\dfrac{87}{522}$

(q)

$\boxed{8}\,)\,\dfrac{77}{616}$

(r)

$\boxed{9}\,)\,\dfrac{91}{819}$

4. Find the quotient and remainder for each of the following.

(a)

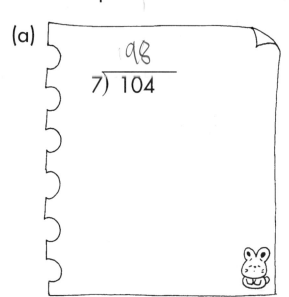

```
    98
7) 104
```

Quotient: 98

Remainder: 6

(b)

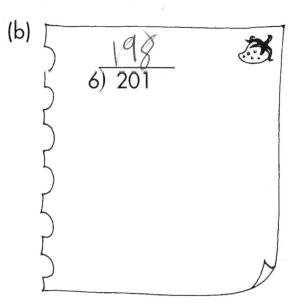

```
    198
6) 201
```

Quotient: 198

Remainder: 3

(c)

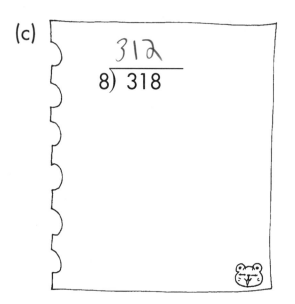

```
    312
8) 318
```

Quotient: 312

Remainder: 6

(d)

```
    89
9) 803
```

Quotient: 89

Remainder: 2

32

(e)

$$
\begin{array}{r}
63 \\
8\overline{)505}
\end{array}
$$

Quotient: 63

Remainder: 1

(f)

$$
\begin{array}{r}
74 \\
6\overline{)446}
\end{array}
$$

Quotient: 74

Remainder: 2

(g)

$$
\begin{array}{r}
71 \\
7\overline{)499}
\end{array}
$$

Quotient: 71

Remainder: 2

(h)

$$
\begin{array}{r}
92 \\
8\overline{)741}
\end{array}
$$

Quotient: 92

Remainder: 5

(i)

$$93$$
$$6)\overline{563}$$

(j)

$$103$$
$$9)\overline{928}$$

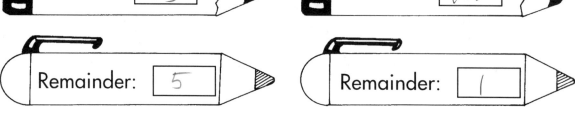

Quotient: 93

Remainder: 5

Quotient: 103

Remainder: 1

Work out the following sums in the space provided. Show all your working and steps clearly.

5. 126 children sat in 9 rows.
    Each row had the same number of children.
    How many children sat in each row?

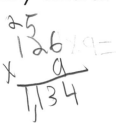

Answer:

6. John sold 6 crates of fruits.
   There were 120 fruits in each crate.
   How many fruits did he sell?

   $$\begin{array}{r} 120 \\ \times\ \ 6 \\ \hline 720 \end{array}$$

   Answer: | 720 |

7. There are 270 letters in two bags.
   Bag A has 20 letters more than Bag B.
   How many letters are there in Bag A?

   $$\begin{array}{r} 270 \\ \times\ 20 \\ \hline 000 \\ +540 \\ \hline 5400 \end{array}$$

   Answer: | 5,400 |

8. In a class there were 20 children.
   The teacher distributed 3 sweets to each child.
   She had 5 sweets left.
   How many sweets did she have at first?

   $$\begin{array}{r} 20 \\ \times\ 3 \\ \hline 60 \end{array}$$

   Answer: | 60 |

9. Mr Chu picked 455 rambutans.
   His wife picked only 145 rambutans.
   They put these rambutans equally into 8 baskets.
   How many rambutans were there in each basket?

   $$\begin{array}{r} 455 \\ +145 \\ \hline 600 \end{array}$$

   Answer: | 75 |

10. Mr Jamil had 856 durians.
    40 of them were rotten.
    He packed the rest into baskets of 6.
    How many baskets of durians were there?

$$856 - 40 = 816$$

Answer: 136

11. A fruit seller packed 275 oranges into bags of 7.
    (a) How many bags were there?
    (b) How many oranges were left over?

Answer: (a)

Answer: (b)

12. Mr Fu owns 6 factories.
    275 people work in each factory.
    40 people in each factory are supervisors.
    How many people in the 6 factories are not supervisors?

Answer:

REVISION 2

Name: _____

Date: _____

Time allowed: 1 h 30 min

Section A (20 × 2 marks)

Choose the correct answer and write its number in the brackets provided.

1. Which of the following numbers is the greatest?
   (1) 2 946   (2) 2 649
   (3) 2 496   (4) 2 964   ( )

2. 2 020 written in words is _____.
   (1) two thousand and two
   (2) two thousand and twenty
   (3) two thousand and two hundred
   (4) two thousand and twelve   ( )

3. 9 497 = 9 000 + ☐ + 90 + 7.
   The missing number in the box is _____.
   (1) 4 000   (2) 400
   (3) 40   (4) 4   ( )

4. The number that is 1 more than 9 999 is _____.
   (1) 1 000   (2) 9 989
   (3) 9 998   (4) 10 000   ( )

5. What does the digit 7 in 7 459 stand for?
   (1) 7 ones   (2) 7 tens
   (3) 7 hundreds   (4) 7 thousands   ( )

6. In $6 + 6 + 6 + 6 + 6 = \boxed{} \times 6$, the missing number in the box is _____.
   (1) 5   (2) 6   (3) 30   (4) 36   ( )

7. When I say "16, 20, 24, 28, ...", I am counting in _____.
   (1) tens   (2) eights
   (3) fours   (4) twos   ( )

8. $24 \div 4$ is the same as _____.
   (1) 2×3 (2) 2×4
   (3) 2×6 (4) 3×6 ( )

9. What is the next number in the number pattern?

   $$63, 56, \boxed{}, 42.$$

   (1) 7   (2) 49
   (3) 53   (4) 55   ( )

10. The value of 34×4 is _____.
    (1) 128   (2) 136
    (3) 181   (4) 1 216   ( )

11. In $8 + 6 = 7 \boxed{} 2$, the missing sign in the box is _____.
    (1) +   (2) –   (3) $\div$ (4) $\times$ ( )

12. Which one of the following has the same result as 4×3?
    (1) $3 + 4$ (2) 3×4
    (3) $4 - 3$ (4) $4 \div 3$ ( )

13. $9 \times 4 = 32 + \boxed{}$.
    The missing number in the box is _____.
    (1) 9   (2) 8   (3) 6   (4) 4   ( )

14. How many fives are there in sixty?

(1) 9   (2) 10   (3) 11   (4) 12   ( )

15. Which one of the following numbers when divided by 8 will give a remainder?

(1) 32   (2) 48   (3) 57   (4) 64   ( )

16. 9 pupils shared 63 pencils equally among themselves. How many pencils did each pupil get?

(1) 7   (2) 54   (3) 81   (4) 567   ( )

17. One exercise book has 34 pages. Another exercise book has 16 pages more. How many pages are there in the 2 exercise books?

(1) 32   (2) 50   (3) 74   (4) 84   ( )

18. 56 sweets are to be shared equally among 8 children. Which one of the following methods will you use to find the number of sweets each child will get?

(1) $56 + 8$ (2) 56×8

(3) $56 - 8$ (4) $56 \div 8$ ( )

19. The value of $134 \div 6$ is _____.

(1) 15 remainder 1   (2) 13 remainder 11

(3) 22 remainder 2   (4) 12 remainder 2   ( )

20. The product of 350 and 7 is _____.

(1) 2 540   (2) 2 450

(3) 357   (4) 343   ( )

Section B (20 × 2 marks)

Write your answers in the boxes provided.

21. $3\,000 + 40 + 7 = \boxed{}$

22. $\boxed{} - 1\,256 = 3\,214$

23. $35 \div 7 = 28 \div 7 + \boxed{}$

24. $10 \times 10 = 9 \times 10 + \boxed{}$

25. $\boxed{}$ is 100 more than 2 999.

26. $10 \times 0 = \boxed{}$

27. $64 \div 8 = 4 \boxed{} 4$. The missing sign in the box is $\boxed{}$.

28. 5 thousands 6 hundreds 8 ones $= \boxed{}$

29. 4 hundreds $= \boxed{}$ tens

30. 5 tens $\times 10 = \boxed{}$

31. 6 hundreds $\div 10 = \boxed{}$ tens

32. $9\,000 - \boxed{} = 2\,400$

40

33. Ali has twice as many marbles as John.
    If Ali has 250 marbles, how many marbles does John have?

    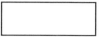

34. 910 books were shared equally among 7 classes.

    How many books did each class get?

35. Write >, < or = in the box.

    $90 \div 3$ [   ] 10×4

36. Mrs Lin used 3 kg of flour to make cakes.
    She used 15 eggs for every kilogram of flour.

    How many eggs did Mrs Lin use?

    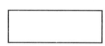

37. John has 120 marbles.
    James has 20 less marbles than John.
    How many marbles must John give to James so that they will have

    the same number of marbles?

38. The numbers in the diagram are related. What is the missing number
    in the box?

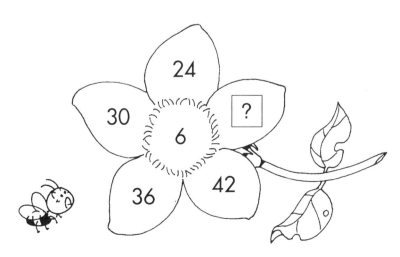

39.
$$35 \div 7 = 5$$
$$40 \div 8 = 5$$
$$\boxed{} \div 9 = 5$$

The missing number in the box is $\boxed{}$.

40. The difference between two numbers is 446.
If the greater number is 1 044, what is the other number?

Section C (5 × 4 marks)

Work out the following sums in the space provided. Show all your working and steps clearly.

41. An angsana tree has 1 408 leaves.
There are 645 fewer leaves in a bougainvillea.
How many leaves are there in the bougainvillea?

Answer: $\boxed{}$

42. A multi-storey car park can hold 1 200 cars.
On a certain day, there were 486 cars parked there.
How many empty lots were there on that day?

Answer: $\boxed{}$

43. Mrs Rama has 600 eggs. She put 8 eggs in each box. If 120 eggs are broken, how many boxes will she need?

Answer:

44. There are 550 carnations and twice as many orchids in a nursery. How many carnations and orchids are there altogether?

Answer:

45. Mr Chen had 3 000 guppies and goldfish altogether.
He sold some of them and had 850 guppies and 280 goldfish left.
How many guppies and goldfish did Mr Chen sell altogether?

Answer:

Name: _____

Date: _____

Marks:

/100

Time allowed: 1 h 30 min

Section A (20 × 2 marks)

Choose the correct answer and write its number in the brackets provided.

1. The place value of the digit 5 in the numeral 2 568 is _____.
    (1) ones   (2) tens
    (3) hundreds   (4) thousands   ( )

2. 9 thousands, 6 tens and 8 ones written as a numeral is _____.
    (1) 9 068   (2) 9 086
    (3) 9 680   (4) 9 868   ( )

3. 8 888 = 8 000 + ☐ + 88
    (1) 8   (2) 80   (3) 800   (4) 808   ( )

4. 5 000 + 200 + 30 + 5 is the same as _____.
    (1) 5 235   (2) 5 325
    (3) 5 352   (4) 5 523   ( )

5. In 6 407, the digit 4 stands for _____.
    (1) 4×1 (2) 4×10
    (3) 4×100 (4) $4 \times 1\ 000$ ( )

6. The number between 499 and 501 is _____.
    (1) 498   (2) 500   (3) 502   (4) 510   ( )

44

7. Which of the following has the same value as 6 hundreds 6 tens and 10 ones?
    (1) 7 000   (2) 6 610
    (3) 670   (4) 661   (   )

8. Which one of the following does **not** have the same value as 100?
    (1) 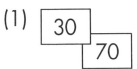   (2)

    (3) 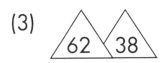   (4) 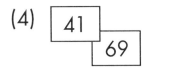   (   )

9. Which of the following is 7 less than 1 000?
    (1) 700   (2) 903
    (3) 970   (4) 993   (   )

10. 4 × 9 has the same value as _____.
    (1) 4 + 4 + 4 + 4   (2) 4 × 4 × 4 × 4
    (3) 9 + 9 + 9 + 9   (4) 9 × 9 × 9 × 9   (   )

11. 5 068 is 100 more than _____.
    (1) 4 068   (2) 4 968
    (3) 5 168   (4) 6 068   (   )

12. Which of the following is **not equal** to 1 000?
    (1) 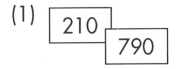   (2)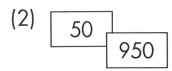

    (3) 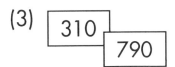   (4)   (   )

45

13. Ali counts, "12, 16, 20, 24, 28 ...".
    He is counting in _____.
    (1) fives   (2) fours
    (3) threes   (4) twos   ( )

14. $5\,000 - 1\,800 = 1\,200 +$ ☐.

    The missing number in the box is _____.
    (1) 3 200   (2) 3 000
    (3) 2 000   (4) 200   ( )

15. The missing number in the number pattern shown below is _____.

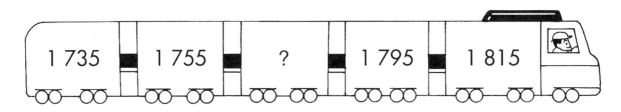

    (1) 1 785   (2) 1 775
    (3) 1 765   (4) 1 745   ( )

16. Which one of the following is **incorrect**?
    (1) $10 \times 10 = 100$ (2) $6 \times 4 = 4 \times 6$
    (3) $45 \div 3 = 15$ (4) $45 \div 15 = 5$ ( )

17. ☐ $- 4\,261 = 1\,378$.
    What is the missing number in the box?
    (1) 6 539   (2) 5 639
    (3) 3 882   (4) 2 883   ( )

18. $2 \times 2 =$ ☐ $\div 4$.
    The missing number in the box is _____.
    (1) 20   (2) 16   (3) 12   (4) 8   ( )

46

19. $50 \div 10 = 5 \boxed{} 1$.

The missing sign in the box is _____.

(1) ×   (2) ÷   (3) +   (4) −   (   )

20.

Which of the following is the missing number?

(1) 60   (2) 90   (3) 100   (4) 900   (   )

Section B (20 × 2 marks)

Work out the answer for each question correctly. Write the answer in the box provided.

21. Write eight thousand, three hundred and seventeen in numeral.

22. Form the smallest 3-digit number with the following digits.

23. Form the largest 4-digit number with the following digits.

24. Arrange the following numbers in order, beginning with the **greatest**.

| 503 | 305 | 530 | 350 |

$$\boxed{}, \boxed{}, \boxed{}, \boxed{}.$$

25. Write >, < or = in the box provided.

$$4\,000 + 100 + 8 \quad \boxed{} \quad 4\,000 + 90 + 8$$

26. In 7 608, the value of the digit 7 is 7 × _____. $\boxed{}$

27. 8 × 5 = $\boxed{}$ × 4.

What is the missing number in the box? $\boxed{}$

28. 3 056 + _____ = 5 000.

What is the missing number? $\boxed{}$

29. $\boxed{}$ is 805 less than 2 064.

The missing number in the box is _____. $\boxed{}$

30.
```
    * 564
  +   9**
  ───────
    3 486
```
What number does the '*' stand for? $\boxed{}$

48

31. Find the missing number in the box below.

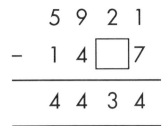

```
    5  9  2  1
 -  1  4 [ ] 7
 _____
    4  4  3  4
 _____
```

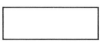

32.

 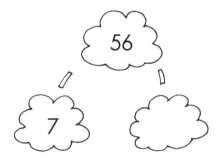

What is the missing number in the above?

33. What is the missing number in the box?

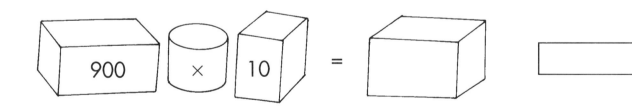

34. Find the remainder when 675 is divided by 7.

For questions 35 and 36, write >, < or = in the boxes provided.

35. $300 \div 6$ ◯ $100 \div 2$

36. 100×10 ◯ 300×5

37. A number when divided by 3 has a quotient of 301 and a remainder of 2. What is the number?

38. Find the value of 697 × 3.

39. [| × 4] = [1 020]

What is the missing number?

40.

```
              ┌──────┐
              │  24  │
              ├──────┤
              │   4  │
       ┌──────┼──────┼──────┬──────┐
       │  12  │   2  │      │   8  │  48  │
       └──────┼──────┼──────┴──────┘
              │   6  │
              ├──────┤
              │  36  │
              └──────┘
```

What is the missing number in the box?

Section C (5 × 4 marks)

Work out the following sums in the space provided. Show all your working and steps clearly.

---

41. A fruit seller had 890 oranges.
    He sold some of them.
    If he had 295 oranges left, how many oranges did he sell?

Answer: ☐

---

42. A video cassette recorder costs $440.
    A television set costs 4 times as much as the video cassette recorder.
    How much does the television set cost?

Answer: ☐

43. 1 905 girls and 2 108 boys took part in an art competition. The number of children who took part this year was 600 less than last year. How many children took part in the art competition last year?

Answer:

44. Miss Lim gave some sweets to her class of 40 children. She gave each child 4 sweets and had 15 sweets left. How many sweets did she have at first?

Answer:

45. There are 879 red marbles in a box. The number of red marbles is 3 times the number of green marbles. How many marbles are there in the box altogether?

Answer:

EXERCISE 5

Length

1. Use your ruler to measure the following lines.

(a) A ×————————————× B   AB = _____ cm.

(b) C ×——————————————× D   CD = _____ cm.

(c) E ×
          ╲
            ╲
              × F   EF = _____ cm.

(d)   × H   GH = _____ cm.
          ╱
    G ×

(e) Which line is the longest?   _____

(f) Which line is the shortest?   _____

(g) What is the difference between the longest line and the shortest line?   _____

2. The diagrams below show the heights of 4 children.

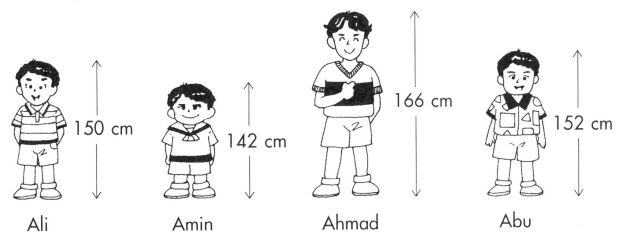

Ali 150 cm   Amin 142 cm   Ahmad 166 cm   Abu 152 cm

53

(a) What is Ali's height? _____

(b) Who is the tallest boy? _____

(c) Who is the shortest boy? _____

(d) What is the difference in height between the tallest boy and the shortest boy? _____

3. Write the missing numbers in the boxes.

(a) 42 cm + [ ] cm = 1 m

(b) 27 cm + [ ] cm = 90 cm

(c) [ ] cm + 28 cm = 1 m

(d) 1 m − [ ] cm = 55 cm

(e) 1 m − 35 cm = [ ] cm

(f) 48 cm + [ ] cm = 85 cm

(g) [ ] cm − 15 cm = 23 cm

(h) 90 cm − [ ] cm = 45 cm

4. Write >, < or = in each ◯.

   (a) 1 m ◯ 40 cm + 50 cm

   (b) 100 cm − 50 cm ◯ 56 cm

   (c) 70 cm + 50 cm ◯ 1 m 20 cm

   (d) 1 m − 45 cm ◯ 50 cm

5. Fill in each blank with the correct answer.

   (a) 1 m 10 cm = _____ cm

   (b) 100 cm = _____ m _____ cm

   (c) 2 m = _____ cm

   (d) 200 cm = _____ m _____ cm

   (e) 2 m 5 cm = _____ cm

   (f) 185 cm = _____ m _____ cm

   (g) 3 m 65 cm = _____ cm

   (h) 235 cm = _____ m _____ cm

6. Add the following.

   (a) 1 m 50 cm + 35 cm = _____ m _____ cm

   (b) 2 m 35 cm + 75 cm = _____ m _____ cm

(c)   4 m + 125 cm = _____ m _____ cm

(d)   150 cm + 250 cm = _____ m _____ cm

(e)   75 cm + 75 cm = _____ m _____ cm

7. Subtract the following.

(a)   1 m − 25 cm = _____ m _____ cm

(b)   2 m 25 cm − 75 cm = _____ m _____ cm

(c)   3 m − 1 m 25 cm = _____ m _____ cm

(d)   2 m − 50 cm = _____ m _____ cm

(e)   4 m − 2 m 75 cm = _____ m _____ cm

8. Write the missing numbers in the blanks.

(a)   1 km 500 m = _____ m

(b)   2 km 200 m = _____ m

(c)   1 750 m = _____ km _____ m

(d)   2 050 m = _____ km _____ m

(e)   1 km 300 m + 700 m = _____ km _____ m

(f)   3 km 340 m + 660 m = _____ km _____ m

(g)   450 m + _____ m = 1 km

(h)   3 km − 2 km 500 m = _____ km _____ m

(i)   1 km − 370 m = _____ km _____ m

(j)   3 km − _____ m = 1 km 500 m

Work out the following problems and write the answers in the boxes provided.

9. Ailing is 1 m 42 cm tall. Aimei is 12 cm taller than Ailing but 5 cm shorter than Aixing.

   (a) How tall is Aixing?

   (b) What is the difference in height between Ailing and Aixing?

   (c) What is the total height of the three girls?

10.

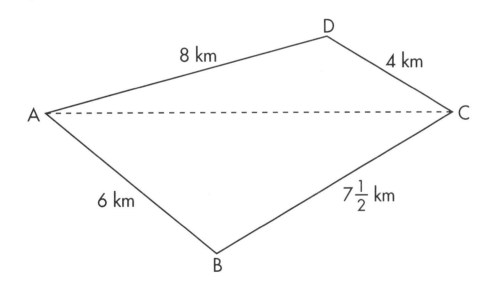

   (a) What is the distance covered if Jiezhi jogs from A to D, D to C, C to B and then B to A? ☐ km

   (b) What is the distance from A to C via D? ☐ km

   (c) Which is the shorter route if Ali decides to travel from B to D, via A or C? ☐

11. The following is the results in a shot putt competition.

Rashid	2 m 80 cm	Ashok	3 m 05 cm
Kumar	2 m 95 cm	Eugene	3 m 10 cm
Limin	2 m 84 cm	John	2 m 89 cm
Kaihong	2 m 99 cm	Jandi	2 m 98 cm

(a) Who was the winner of the event?

(b) How far did Kaihong throw?

(c) Who was the first runner-up?

12.

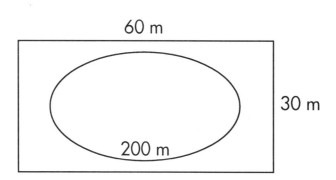

60 m

30 m

200 m

The figure shows a rectangular field and a running track in the field.
Zheyi jogs round the perimeter of the field 3 times.
Eugene jogs round the running track 4 times.

(a) What is the total distance covered by Zheyi?

(b) What is the total distance covered by Eugene?

(c) Who covers more?

How much more?

13. Mother bought 3 m 50 cm of blue ribbon, 3 m of yellow ribbon and 4 m of pink ribbon.

(a) What is the total length of the 3 ribbons?

(b) What is the difference in length between the pink ribbon and the blue ribbon?

(c) If she used 8 m 50 cm of ribbon, how much ribbon had she left?

Do these sums carefully showing all your working and statements.

14.

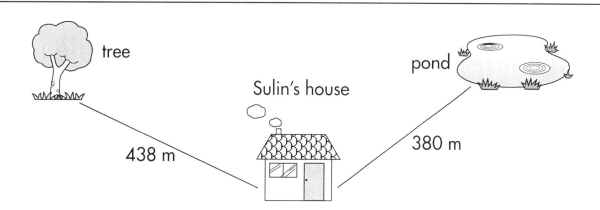

(a) Is the tree or the pond nearer to Sulin's house?
(b) How much nearer is it?

Answer: (a)

(b)

15. Ali used 425 cm of string to tie a parcel.
    John used twice as much string as Ali to tie another parcel.
    What was the length of string John used?

    Answer: [   ]

16. A piece of plank is 1 m 264 cm long.
    It is sawn into 4 equal pieces.
    What is the length of each piece?

    Answer: [   ]

17. Kuala Lumpur is about 328 km away from Singapore. Malacca is
    about 247 km away from Singapore.
    (a) Which town is nearer to Singapore?
    (b) How much nearer is it?

    Answer: (a) [   ]
            (b) [   ]

18. The diagram below shows the approximate distances between some MRT stations in the North.

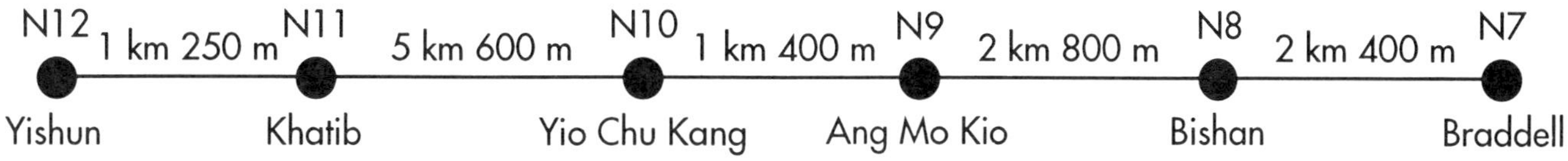

N12 1 km 250 m N11 5 km 600 m N10 1 km 400 m N9 2 km 800 m N8 2 km 400 m N7
●   ●   ●   ●   ●   ●
Yishun   Khatib   Yio Chu Kang   Ang Mo Kio   Bishan   Braddell

Answer the following questions based on the diagram above.

(a) What is the distance between N7 and N12?

[   ] km [   ] m

(b) N9 is [   ] km [   ] m away from N11.

(c) The shortest distance between any two stations is

[   ] km [   ] m.

(d) How far is the Khatib station from Bishan?

[   ] km [   ] m

(e) If you are at N9, how far are you from N12?

[   ] km [   ] m

61

1. Write the weight of each of the following.

(a)

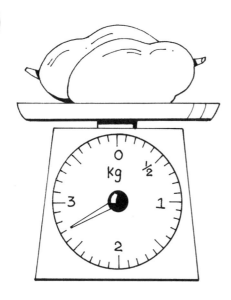

_____ kg _____ g

(b)

_____ kg _____ g

(c)

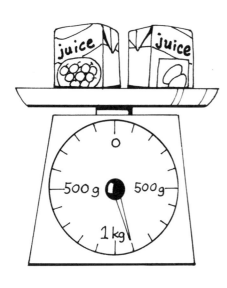

_____ kg _____ g

(d)

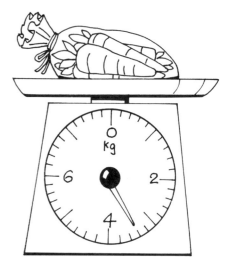

_____ kg _____ g

(e)

(f)

_____ kg _____ g   _____ kg _____ g

2. Write the missing numbers in the boxes.

(a) 300 g + ⬚ g = 1 kg

(b) 1 kg = ⬚ g + 700 g

(c) 1 kg = 234 g + ⬚ g

(d) 1 kg – ⬚ g = 250 g

(e) 1 kg – ⬚ g = 640 g

(f) ⬚ g + 344 g = 1 kg

(g) 2 kg = ⬚ g + 1 kg

(h) ⬚ g + 1 kg 200 g = 3 kg

63

(i) 4 kg + 2 kg 600 g = [   ] kg [   ] g

(j) 6 kg = 2 kg 400 g + [   ] kg [   ] g

3. Fill in the blanks.

(a) 1 kg 300 g = _____ g

(b) 2 800 g = _____ kg _____ g

(c) 2 kg 450 g = _____ g

(d) 3 070 g = _____ kg _____ g

(e) 1 kg 265 g = _____ g

(f) 3 826 g = _____ kg _____ g

(g) 2 kg 805 g = _____ g

(h) 1 400 g = _____ kg _____ g

(i) 3 kg 60 g = _____ g

(j) 4 005 g = _____ kg _____ g

Look at the diagrams carefully and write your answers in the boxes provided.

4.

(a) The total weight of the fruits is [   ] g.

(b) If the orange weighs 150 g, the weight of the 2 apples is [   ] g.

64

5.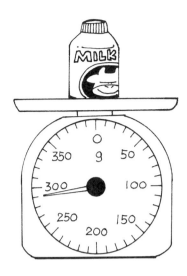

(a) The weight of the bottle of milk is [ ] g.

(b) If the weight of the empty bottle is 110 g, the weight of the milk is [ ] g.

6.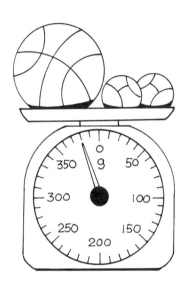

(a) The total weight of the basketball and the 2 tennis balls is [ ] g.

(b) If the basketball weighs 290 g, the weight of the 2 tennis balls is [ ] g.

(c) If every tennis ball weighs the same, the weight of each one is [ ] g.

7.

(a) The total weight of the can and 5 marbles is [ ] g.

(b) The can weighs 190 g, the weight of the 5 marbles is [ ] g.

(c) If the marbles are of the same weight, each marble weighs [ ] g.

8. Study the weights of these items and then fill in the blanks with the correct answers.

(a) The packet of salt and the _____ have the same weight.

(b) The _____ is/are the lightest in weight.

(c) 2 packets of sugar weigh _____ g.

(d) 3 tins of biscuits weigh _____ g.

(e) The total weight of the coffee powder and the biscuits is _____ g.

(f) The box of chocolates is _____ g heavier than the box of tea bags.

(g) 6 tins of coffee powder weigh _____ kg _____ g.

(h) 4 packets of salt are as heavy as _____ packets of sugar.

66

9. Do these sums.

(a)
```
      759 g
  +   309 g
  _____
          g   = _____ kg _____ g
  _____
```

(b)
```
      345 g
  +   655 g
  _____
          g   = _____ kg _____ g
  _____
```

(c)
```
      728 g
  +   874 g
  _____
          g   = _____ kg _____ g
  _____
```

(d)
```
    1 kg   482 g
  + 2 kg   322 g
  _____
      kg       g   = _____ g
  _____
```

(e)
```
    4 kg   163 g
  + 2 kg   795 g
  _____
      kg       g   = _____ g
  _____
```

(f)
```
    3 kg   495 g
  + 5 kg   215 g
  _____
      kg       g   = _____ g
  _____
```

(g)   1 330 g
     − 220 g
     _____
         g   = _____ kg _____ g
     _____

(h)   3 520 g
     − 1 240 g
     _____
         g   = _____ kg _____ g
     _____

(i)   3 000 g
     − 1 728 g
     _____
         g   = _____ kg _____ g
     _____

(j)   258 g
     ×   6
     _____
         g   = _____ kg _____ g
     _____

(k)   309 g
     ×   8
     _____
         g   = _____ kg _____ g
     _____

(l)   1 kg 262 g
     ×   4
     _____
           g   = _____ kg _____ g
     _____

(m)   4)3 348 g   (n)   5)2 650 g

68

Do these sums carefully showing all your working and statements.

10. A baker bought 8 kg of flour. He used 3 kg 360 g to bake cakes. How much flour had he left?

Answer: ☐ kg ☐ g

11. 4 kg 80 g of sugar was packed into packets each weighing 8 g. How many packets of sugar were there?

Answer: ☐

12. A bag of flour weighs 2 kg 500 g.
A bag of potatoes weighs 3 times as much.
How heavy is the bag of potatoes?

Answer: ☐ g

13. Mrs Lim bought 5 kg of sugar.
    She used 2 kg for baking cakes and packed the rest into 5 bags of the same weight.
    What is the weight of each bag of sugar in grams?

    Answer: _____ g

14. A bag of rice weighs 5 kg.
    A bag of sugar weighs 3 kg.
    What is the total weight of 2 bags of rice and 3 bags of sugar?

    Answer: _____ kg

15. Father weighs 70 kg 200 g.
    Mother weighs 12 kg 500 g less.
    What is their total weight?

    Answer: _____ kg _____ g

16. The total weight of Tom and Jerry is 50 kg.
Tom weighs 10 kg more than Jerry.
What is Jerry's weight?

Answer: ⬚ kg ⬚ g

17. Mary's weight is twice Jane's weight.
If their total weight is 60 kg, what is Jane's weight?

Answer: ⬚ kg

18. Suchen weighs 20 kg 650 g.
Her sister weighs 2 kg 350 g more.
What is her sister's weight?

Answer: ⬚ kg ⬚ g

19. A durian weighs 2 kg 250 g.
    A watermelon weighs 800 g less.
    A papaya weighs 400 g less than the watermelon.
    What is the weight of the papaya?

Answer: ☐ kg ☐ g

FIRST SEMESTRAL EXAMINATION

Name: _____

Marks:
| /100 |

Date: _____

Time allowed: 1 h 30 min

Section A (20 × 2 marks)

Choose the correct answer and write its number in the brackets provided.

1. What is 100 more than 1 000?
   - (1) 990
   - (2) 1 010
   - (3) 1 100
   - (4) 1 110 ( )

2. 6 666 is the same as _____.
   - (1) 6 660 + 6
   - (2) 6 606 + 6
   - (3) 6 066 + 6
   - (4) 666 + 6 ( )

3. In 8 406, the digit 4 stands for _____.
   - (1) 4 × 1 000
   - (2) 4 × 100
   - (3) 4 × 10
   - (4) 4 × 1 ( )

4. How many tens are there in 950?
   - (1) 5
   - (2) 9
   - (3) 95
   - (4) 950 ( )

5. ☐ + 189 = 1 000.
   The missing number in the box is _____.
   - (1) 801
   - (2) 810
   - (3) 811
   - (4) 1 189 ( )

6. 7 + 7 + 7 + 7 + 7 is the same as _____.
   - (1) 7 × 7 × 7 × 7 × 7
   - (2) 7 + 5
   - (3) 7 − 5
   - (4) 7 × 5 ( )

7. 52 $\bigcirc$ 4 = 13.

The missing sign in the $\bigcirc$ is _____.
(1) +   (2) −   (3) ×   (4) ÷   (   )

8. 5 m 5 cm is the same as _____ cm.
(1) 55   (2) 505
(3) 550   (4) 5 500   (   )

9. Which of the following is the **shortest** length?
(1) 282 m   (2) 2 m 29 cm
(3) 828 cm   (4) 22 m 8 cm   (   )

10. A packet of nuts weighs 600 g. What is the weight of 10 such packets of nuts?
(1) 6 000 kg   (2) 600 kg
(3) 60 kg   (4) 6 kg   (   )

11. Which of the following numbers can be divided by both 4 and 6 exactly?
(1) 18   (2) 20   (3) 24   (4) 28   (   )

12. $\triangle$ + $\triangle$ + $\triangle$ = 15

$\triangle$ × $\triangle$ = $\boxed{}$

What is the missing number in the box?
(1) 5   (2) 15   (3) 25   (4) 30   (   )

13. $\stackrel{\star}{}$ × 8 = 32

$\boxed{}$ × $\stackrel{\star}{}$ = 36

The missing number in the box is _____.
(1) 9   (2) 8   (3) 7   (4) 6   (   )

14. 3 boys share 90 marbles equally.
    How many marbles will each boy get if each of them is given another 3 marbles?
    (1) 13   (2) 23   (3) 33   (4) 43   (   )

15. 300 children took part in an art competition.
    120 of them were girls.
    How many more boys than girls were there?
    (1) 180   (2) 100   (3) 80   (4) 60   (   )

16. A number when divided by 7 gives a quotient of 11 and a remainder of 3. What is the number?
    (1) 80   (2) 79   (3) 78   (4) 77   (   )

17. Roy bought some magazines at $7 each.
    He gave the cashier $100 and received a change of $44.
    How many magazines did he buy?
    (1) 5   (2) 6   (3) 7   (4) 8   (   )

18. The weight of the basketball is the same as _____ tennis balls.

    (1) 6   (2) 5   (3) 4   (4) 3   (   )

19. If each piece of butter weighs 250 g, what is the weight of the packet of flour?
    (1) 1 200 g
    (2) 1 020 g
    (3) 1 002 g
    (4) 1 000 g

    (   )

20. A doll and a toy car cost $40.
The doll cost 4 times as much as the toy car.
How much did the toy car cost?
(1) $5   (2) $8   (3) $10   (4) $160   (   )

Section B (20 × 2 marks)

Work out the answer for each question and write it in the box provided.

21. The smallest number that can be formed from the digits below is
_____.

0, 1, 2, 8

22. 36, 30, 24, _____, 12.
The missing number in the number pattern is _____.

23. Four thousand, six hundred and eight written as a numeral is _____.

24. [   ] ÷ 8 = 9.
The missing number in the box is _____.

25. 810 = [   ] nines.

26. 1 m 45 cm + [   ] cm = 3 m

27. 8 500 is _____ more than 8 000.

28. $600 \times 5 = \boxed{}$.

What is the missing number in the box?

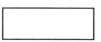

29. $\boxed{} \div 10 = 10$.

The missing number in the box is _____.

30. $\boxed{} + 2\ 468 = 9\ 000$.

The missing number in the box is _____.

31. What is the quotient of $721 \div 7$?

32. 70 pencils are put into boxes of 6.
How many pencils will be left over?

33. $3 \times 5 = \boxed{} \div 2$.

The missing number in the box is _____.

34. ⃝ ⃝ ⃝ ⃝ ⃝ ⃝ ⃝ stand for 616 eggs.

⃝ stands for _____ eggs.

35. Mrs Bala cuts 50 cm of cloth from 2 m of cloth.
How much cloth is left?

36. What is 250 g more than 3 kg 150 g?

$\boxed{}$ kg $\boxed{}$ g

77

37. A papaya weighs 4 times as much as a mango.
    If the mango weighs 225 g, find the weight of the papaya.

    [ ] g

38. What is the weight of the fruits?

    [ ] kg [ ] g

39. Mr Mak sold 9 000 tickets on Monday.
    He sold 2 085 more tickets on Monday than on Tuesday.
    How many tickets did he sell on Tuesday?

    [ ]

40. YX is a 2-digit number. After it is multiplied by 3, 46 is added to it
    to give a total of 100. What number does YX stand for?

    [ ]

Section C (5 × 4 marks)

Work out the following sums in the space provided. Show all your working and steps clearly.

41. Lihua and Liyi together have 2 640 rubber bands.
    Lihua has 1 382 rubber bands.
    How many rubber bands does Liyi have?

    Answer: [ ]

42. Jaslee runs round a track 4 times.
    He runs 1 600 m. How long is the track?

    Answer: [   ]

43. There are 406 pencils in a box.
    How many pencils are there in 7 such boxes?

    Answer: [   ]

44. An egg seller has 700 eggs.
    He put 8 eggs in one tray.
    If 52 eggs are broken, how many trays will he need?

    Answer: [   ]

45. David, John, Ravi and Faizul bought a birthday present.
The present cost $62 and the wrapping paper cost $2.
They shared the cost equally.
How much did Ravi pay?

Answer: _____

— *Word Problems* —

Write the missing numbers in the boxes and then solve the sums, showing all your steps and working.

1.

> There are 420 girls in the hall.
> There are 30 more boys than girls.

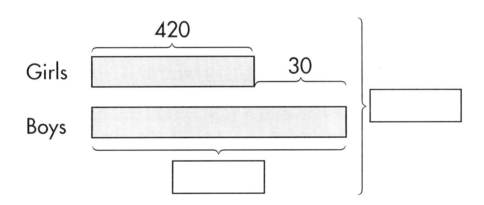

(a) How many boys are there?

[___] + [___] = [___]

There are _____ boys.

(b) How many children are there in the hall?

[___] + [___] = [___]

There are _____ children in the hall.

(c) If 48 children leave the hall, how many children are left?

$$\boxed{} - \boxed{} = \boxed{}$$

_____ children are left.

2.

> A toy car costs $25.
> A train set costs 3 times as much as the toy car.

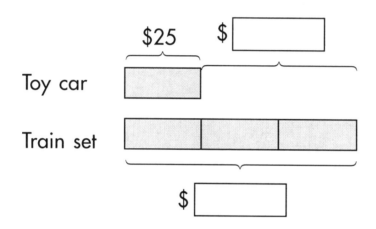

$25 $ $\boxed{}$

Toy car

Train set

$ $\boxed{}$

(a) How much does the train set cost?

$$\boxed{} + \boxed{} = \$ \boxed{}$$

The train set costs $_____.

(b) How much more does the train set cost than the toy car?

$$\boxed{} - \boxed{} = \$ \boxed{}$$

The train set costs $_____ more than the toy car.

3.

> A primary school has 32 rooms.
> The number of classrooms is 3 times the number of special rooms.

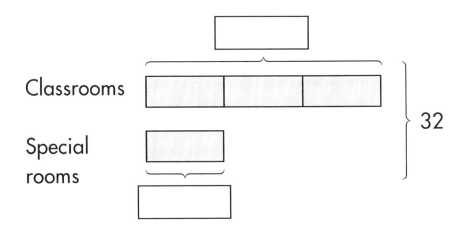

4 units ⟶ 32

1 unit ⟶ ?

(a) How many special rooms are there?

[   ] ÷ [   ] = [   ]

There are _____ special rooms.

(b) How many classrooms are there?

[   ] × [   ] = [   ]

There are _____ classrooms.

4.

> Mrs Wu had $100.
> After paying for 4 kg of crabs, she had $12 left.
> Find the cost of 1 kg of crabs.

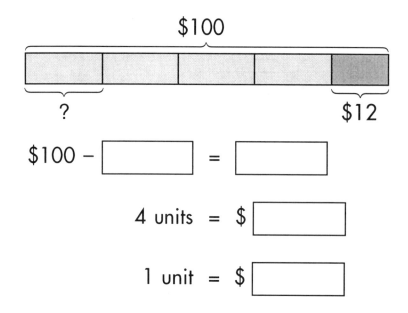

$100 − ⬚ = ⬚

4 units = $ ⬚

1 unit = $ ⬚

1 kg of crabs cost $_____.

5.

> Michael bought a box of 500-piece jigsaw puzzle.
> He completed 86 pieces on the first day and 75 pieces on the second day.
> How many pieces had he left?

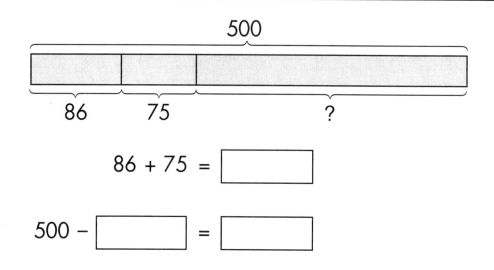

86 + 75 = ⬚

500 − ⬚ = ⬚

He had _____ pieces left.

6.

A farmer had 2 855 eggs.
He broke 28 eggs and sold 1 756 of them.
How many eggs were left?

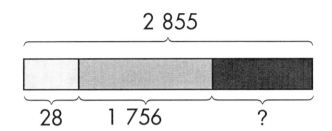

$$28 + 1\ 756 = \boxed{}$$

$$2\ 855 - \boxed{} = \boxed{}$$

_____ eggs were left.

7.

Mr Rahman paid $1 300 for a table and 6 similar chairs. If the table cost $352, how much did each chair cost?

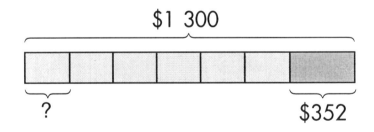

$$\$1\ 300 - \$\boxed{} = \$\boxed{}$$

$$\$\boxed{} \div 6 = \$\boxed{}$$

Each chair cost $_____.

8.

> Jason has 4 albums with 50 photographs in each album.
> Kaiming has 40 more photographs than Jason.
> How many photographs does Kaiming have?

Jason

50

Kaiming

40

$50 \times \boxed{} = \boxed{}$

$40 + \boxed{} = \boxed{}$

Kaiming has _____ photographs.

Do these sums carefully showing all your working and statements.

9. In a class there are 42 pupils.
   There are 8 more boys than girls.
   How many girls are there in the class?

Answer: $\boxed{}$

86

10. John had 48 marbles.

    James had 12 marbles more than John.

    Jerry had twice as many marbles as James.

    How many marbles did Jerry have?

    Answer: [ ]

11. Lily has 65 beads.

    She gives 15 beads to Lilian.

    They have the same number of beads now.

    How many beads does Lilian have at first?

    Answer: [ ]

12. Mother made some sandwiches for a picnic.
Mary ate 4 pieces and Sam ate 3 more pieces than Mary.
Mother and Father ate 3 pieces each.
How many sandwiches did Mother make?

Answer:

13. A farmer collected 86 eggs.
He broke 4 eggs and put the rest of the eggs in trays.
(a) If each tray could hold 10 eggs, how many trays would be needed?
(b) How many eggs were left over?

Answer: (a)

(b)

—————— *Mental Calculation* ——————

1. Write the missing numbers in the boxes.

(a) 52 —— + 40 ——→ ☐

(b) 146 —— + 20 ——→ ☐

(c) 286 —— + 20 ——→ ☐

(d) 86 —— − 30 ——→ ☐ —— − 4 ——→ ☐

86 − 34 = ☐

(e) 196 —— − 50 ——→ ☐ —— − 3 ——→ ☐

196 − 53 = ☐

(f) 200 —— − 40 ——→ ☐ —— − 8 ——→ ☐

200 − 48 = ☐

185 + 15 = 200

(g) 1 000 —— − 200 ——→ ☐ —— − 10 ——→ ☐ —— − 4 ——→ ☐

1 000 − 214 = ☐

(h) 185 —— + 15 ——→ ☐ —— + 43 ——→ ☐

185 + 15 + 43 = ☐

(i) $375 \xrightarrow{+25} \boxed{} \xrightarrow{+82} \boxed{}$

$375 + 25 + 82 = \boxed{}$

(j) $445 \xrightarrow{+55} \boxed{} \xrightarrow{+64} \boxed{}$

$445 + 55 + 64 = \boxed{}$

(k) $870 \xrightarrow{-30} \boxed{} \xrightarrow{-4} \boxed{}$

$870 - 34 = \boxed{}$

(l) $790 \xrightarrow{-70} \boxed{} \xrightarrow{-9} \boxed{}$

$790 - 79 = \boxed{}$

(m) $640 \xrightarrow{-40} \boxed{} \xrightarrow{-9} \boxed{}$

$640 - 49 = \boxed{}$

(n) $908 \xrightarrow{-8} \boxed{} \xrightarrow{-30} \boxed{}$

$908 - 38 = \boxed{}$

(o) $635 \xrightarrow{+65} \boxed{} \xrightarrow{+25} \boxed{}$

$635 + 90 = \boxed{}$

(p) $448 \xrightarrow{+52} \boxed{} \xrightarrow{+13} \boxed{}$

$448 + 65 = \boxed{}$

2. Match the flowers and the butterflies.

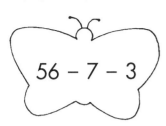 56 – 7 – 3

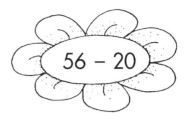 56 – 20

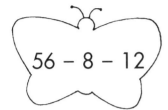 56 – 8 – 12

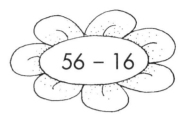 56 – 16

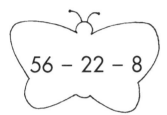 56 – 22 – 8

 56 – 10

56 – 10 – 6

 56 – 17

56 – 41 – 9

 56 – 30

56 – 11 – 4

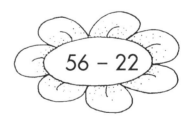 56 – 22

56 – 15 – 7

 56 – 15

56 – 13 – 4

 56 – 50

3. Find the value of each of the following by filling in the missing numbers in the boxes.

(a) $70 - 4 - 6 = 70 - \boxed{}$

$= \boxed{}$

(b) $140 - 13 - 7 = 140 - \boxed{}$

$= \boxed{}$

(c) $238 - 12 - 18 = 238 - \boxed{}$

$= \boxed{}$

(d) $540 - 199 = 340 + \boxed{} - 199$

$= 340 + \boxed{}$

$= \boxed{}$

(e) $467 - 299 = 167 + \boxed{} - 299$

$= 167 + \boxed{}$

$= \boxed{}$

(f) $307 - 99 = 207 + 100 - \boxed{}$

$= 207 + \boxed{}$

$= \boxed{}$

(g) $500 - 198 = 300 + \boxed{} - 198$

$ = 300 + \boxed{}$

$ = \boxed{}$

(h) $356 - 78 = 200 + \boxed{} - 78$

$ = \boxed{} + \boxed{}$

$ = \boxed{}$

(i) $603 - 165 = 403 + \boxed{} - 165$

$ = \boxed{} + \boxed{}$

$ = \boxed{}$

(j) $917 - 674 = 217 + \boxed{} - 674$

$ = \boxed{} + \boxed{}$

$ = \boxed{}$

EXERCISE 9

Money

1. Count the amount of money shown and write the answer in each blank.

(a)
      = $_____

(b)
     = $_____

(c)
      = $_____

(d)
   = $_____

(e)
    = $_____

(f)
    = $_____

RC/27/96-03

2. Fill in the number of notes and coins to make up the given sum of money. Use the highest value. See the example given.

	$10	$5	$1	50¢	20¢	10¢	5¢
$3.60			3	1		1	
$4.55							
$5.90							
$6.15							
$7.35							
$8.75							
$5.25							
$12.10							
$13.70							
$25.20							
$32.65							
$26.30							

3. Fill in the boxes with the correct answers.

(a) Eighty-five cents = $ [   ]

(b) Two dollars and eight cents = $ [   ]

(c) Twelve dollars and forty cents = $ [   ]

95

4. Write each amount of money in words.

(a) $0.45	
(b) $5.80	
(c) $10.06	
(d) $386	
(e) $1 588	
(f) $6 514	

5. Fill in the blanks.

(a) 125¢ = $_____   (b) $0.25 = _____¢

(c) 340¢ = $_____   (d) $6.70 = _____¢

(e) 1 670¢ = $_____   (f) $11.05 = _____¢

(g) 3 905¢ = $_____   (h) $22.80 = _____¢

6. Write the missing numbers.

(a)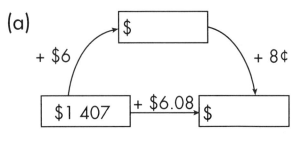

(b)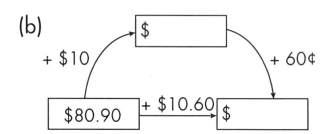

96

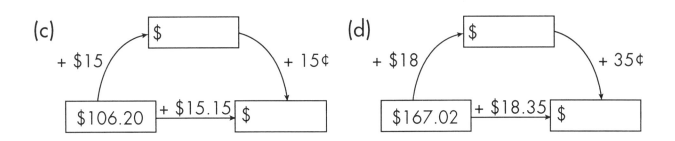

(c) + $15 → $ [ ] + 15¢ → $106.20 + $15.15 → $ [ ]

(d) + $18 → $ [ ] + 35¢ → $167.02 + $18.35 → $ [ ]

(e) Fifty dollars and twenty cents = $ [ ]

(f) Three hundred and five dollars and nine cents = $ [ ]

(g) Two thousand and fifty-eight dollars = $ [ ]

7. Do these sums.

(a)   60¢
   +   45¢
   _____
        ¢ = $_____
   _____

(b)   85¢
   +   75¢
   _____
        ¢ = $_____
   _____

(c)   90¢
   +   80¢
   _____
        ¢ = $_____
   _____

(d)   95¢
   +   55¢
   _____
        ¢ = $_____
   _____

8. Add.

(a) $3.50 + $2.40	(b) $4.65 + $3.25	(c) $8.45 + $1.95
(d) $15.40 + $12.90	(e) $25.75 + $24.25	(f) $34.95 + $65.05

9. Write the missing numbers.

(a)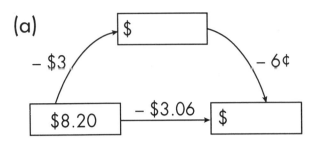

(b)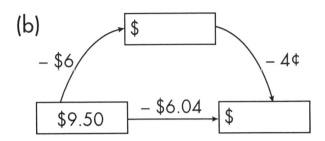

(c)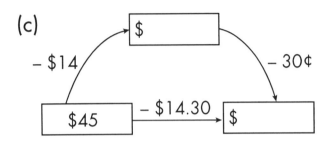

(d)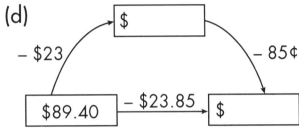

10. Subtract.

(a) $50.80 − $17.25	(b) $36.90 − $15.70	(c) $88.98 − $18.06
(d) $68.02 − $41.55	(e) $94.62 − $89.78	(f) $100.00 − $ 87.64

11. Multiply.

(a) $0.75 × 2	(b) $1.08 × 3	(c) $5.06 × 10

(d) $9.50
  $\times$ 4
_____
 	
_____
	(e) $0.77
	  $\times$ 5
	_____
	
	_____
		(f) $3.45
		  $\times$ 8
		_____
		
		_____

(g) $2.48
  $\times$ 6
_____
 	
_____
	(h) $7.80
	  $\times$ 7
	_____
	
	_____
		(i) $4.90
		  $\times$ 9
		_____
		
		_____

12. Divide.

(a) $4\overline{)\$8.00}$	(b) $3\overline{)\$9.27}$	(c) $2\overline{)\$0.60}$
(d) $5\overline{)\$8.80}$	(e) $6\overline{)\$2.58}$	(f) $8\overline{)\$5.60}$
(g) $7\overline{)\$7.63}$	(h) $9\overline{)\$6.03}$	(i) $8\overline{)\$1.04}$

13. Study the price tags and complete the following bills.

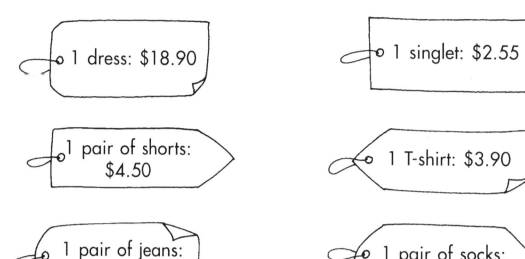

(a) Mr Li's Bill	(b) Miss Chen's Bill
1 T-shirt = $_____	1 dress = $_____
1 pair of jeans = $_____	1 pair of shorts = $_____
Total: = $_____	Total: = $_____
Money given: = $50.00	Money given: = $30.00
Change: = $_____	Change: = $_____
(c) Mr Wang's Bill	**(d) Mrs Fu's Bill**
2 singlets = $_____	2 dresses = $_____
2 T-shirts = $_____	2 pairs of socks = $_____
1 pair of shorts = $_____	1 pair of jeans = $_____
Total: = $_____	Total: = $_____
Money given: = $20.00	Money given: = $100.00
Change: = $_____	Change: = $_____

100

Do these sums carefully showing all your working and statements.

14. Mother spent $4.50 on meat, $7.80 on fish and $3.20 on vegetables. How much did she spend altogether?

Answer:

15. A book cost $3.95.
Weiliang bought 8 such books.
How much did he spend?

Answer:

16. Father bought a clock for $52.50.
He gave the salesman a $100 note.
How much change did he get back?

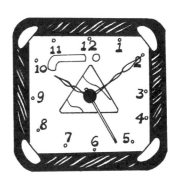

Answer:

17. 9 similar game sets cost $80.10.
    Find the cost of each game set.

Answer:

18. I paid $5.00 for a T-shirt and $4.50 for a pair of socks.
    How much did I pay altogether?

$5.00

$4.50

Answer:

19. I paid $1.30 for a toothbrush and $2.25 for a tube of toothpaste.
    How much did I pay for the two articles?

$1.30

$2.25

Answer:

20. I paid $0.35 for an orange and $1.85 for a papaya.
    How much did I pay if I bought 6 oranges and the papaya?

    Answer: [ ]

21. Mary saves $8.50 a week.
    How much will she save in 9 weeks?

    Answer: [ ]

22. Tom and Tim bought a present which cost $18.60.
    They shared the cost equally.
    How much did each boy pay?

    Answer: [ ]

23. I bought a bag for $14.50. I gave the salesman $50.
    How much change did I get?

    Answer: [   ]

24. 1 apple cost 30 cents. I bought 4 such apples.
    (a) How much did I pay for the 4 apples?
    (b) I gave the fruit seller $2.00. How much change would I get?

    Answer: (a) [   ]
            (b) [   ]

25. 1 loaf of bread cost $1.50. I bought 2 such loaves.
    How much change would I get if I paid the baker $10.00?

    Answer: [   ]

REVISION 3

Name: _____

Date: _____

Marks:
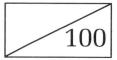
/100

Time allowed: 1 h 30 min

Section A (20 × 2 marks)

Choose the correct answer and write its number in the brackets provided.

1. The digit 6 in 1 607 stands for _____.
   (1) 6 × 1 000   (2) 6 × 100
   (3) 6 × 10   (4) 6 × 1   (   )

2. 1 000 + 30 + 4 is the same as _____.
   (1) 1 034   (2) 1 043
   (3) 1 304   (4) 1 403   (   )

3. The missing number in the pattern below is _____.

   77, 84, [   ], 98

   (1) 85   (2) 87   (3) 91   (4) 97   (   )

4. 3 × 5 is the same as _____.
   (1) 5 + 5 + 5 + 5 + 5   (2) 3 + 3 + 3
   (3) 5 + 5 + 5   (4) 5 + 3 + 5 + 3 + 5   (   )

5. 56 × 8 is the same as _____.
   (1) 484   (2) 458   (3) 448   (4) 408   (   )

6. If ○ stands for 5 eggs, which one of the following sets shows 30 eggs?
   (1) ○ ○ ○   (2) ○ ○ ○ ○
   (3) ○ ○ ○ ○ ○   (4) ○ ○ ○ ○ ○ ○   (   )

105

7. An egg seller had 564 eggs. He sold 195 eggs.
   How many eggs had he left?
   (1) 759   (2) 469
   (3) 431   (4) 369   (   )

8. In the figure, the shortest line joining P and Q is _____.
   (1) line A
   (2) line B
   (3) line C
   (4) line D   (   )

9. 307 cents is the same as _____.
   (1) $30.70   (2) $30.07
   (3) $3.70   (4) $3.07   (   )

10. 3 m 5 cm = [   ] cm.
    The missing number in the box is _____.
    (1) 305   (2) 350
    (3) 3 005   (4) 3 500   (   )

11. What is the weight of the fruits?
    (1) 302 g

    (2) 320 g

    (3) 3 012 g

    (4) 3 020 g   (   )

12. Derong has five 20-cent coins and four 10-cent coins. He has _____
    altogether.
    (1) 29 cents   (2) 30 cents
    (3) $1.04   (4) $1.40   (   )

13. What is the total sum of these coins and the note?

| $5 | 50¢ | 20¢ | 20¢ | 10¢ | 5¢ |

    (1) $5.85   (2) $5.95
    (3) $6.05   (4) $6.50   (   )

14. $3 − ☐ = $1.35.
What is the missing number in the box?
    (1) $1.55   (2) $1.65
    (3) $2.55   (4) $2.75   (   )

15. $15.70 + $20.30 = _____
    (1) $36.10   (2) $36.00
    (3) $35.10   (4) $35.00   (   )

16. 2 000 cents is the same as _____.
    (1) $2.00   (2) $20.00
    (3) $200.00   (4) $2 000.00   (   )

17. Mariam paid $6.75 for 3 files.
How much did 1 file cost?
    (1) $9.75   (2) $3.75
    (3) $3.25   (4) $2.25   (   )

18. A toy truck costs $8.90.
A musical box costs 3 times as much as the toy truck.
What is the cost of the musical box?
    (1) $26.70   (2) $26.10
    (3) $11.90   (4) $5.90   (   )

19. Arif's father gave him $10.
His mother gave him $8.
He spent $9.30 on some story books.
How much money had he left?
    (1) $27.30   (2) $9.70
    (3) $8.70   (4) $7.30   (   )

20. At a sale, toothbrushes are sold at 2 for $3.50 or $2.00 each. Jasmine has $10.
   What is the greatest number of toothbrushes she can buy?
   (1) 4
   (2) 5
   (3) 6
   (4) 7

   2 for $3.50

   ( )

Section B (20 × 2 marks)

Write your answer in the box provided.

21. The largest **odd** number that can be formed with these digits is _____.

   6, 3, 1, 0

22. 5 hundreds × 4 = _____ hundreds

23. Write >, < or = in the box.

   160 ÷ 10 ◯ 8 × 2

24. 475 + [   ] = 639.

   The missing number in the box is _____.

25. 23 × 8 = _____

26. 402 ÷ 6 = _____

27. 168 = [   ] × 3

   The missing number in the box is _____.

28. 6 500 is _____ more than 5 000.

29. The numbers in the diagram are related.
    What is the missing number?

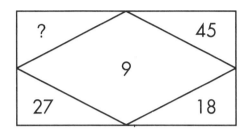

30. What is 500 g more than 3 kg 50 g?

_____ kg _____ g

31. 1 km 590 m + _____ m = 2 km

32. 2 m 35 cm + _____ cm = 4 m

Look at the diagrams below carefully. Use it to answer questions 33 to 37.

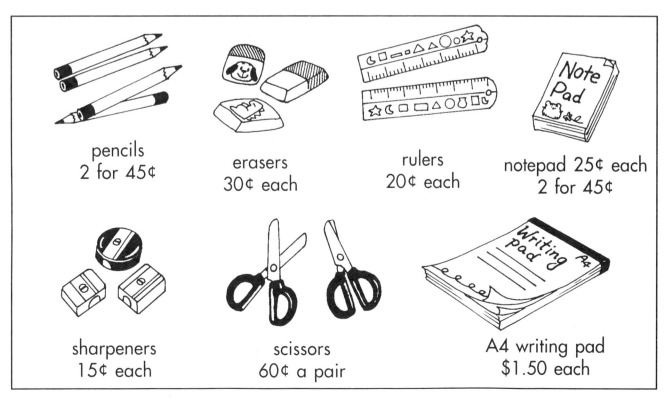

pencils
2 for 45¢

erasers
30¢ each

rulers
20¢ each

notepad 25¢ each
2 for 45¢

sharpeners
15¢ each

scissors
60¢ a pair

A4 writing pad
$1.50 each

33. Johari bought 10 pencils, 2 fancy rulers and 4 sharpeners. How much did he pay altogether?

$ [   ]

34. Meilin bought 2 pairs of scissors and 2 A4 writing pads. She gave the cashier a five-dollar note.

How much change did she receive?

$ [   ]

35. Jerry bought 4 notepads.

How much did he pay for them?

$ [   ]

36. The cost of 4 sharpeners = [   ] erasers.

What is the missing number in the box?

[   ]

37. Miss Lim paid $4.30 for 5 fancy rulers, 10 sharpeners and some notepads. How many notepads did she buy?

[   ]

38. Mrs Wu paid $6 for 4 mangoes.

How much did one mango cost?

[   ]

39. $20.00 = [   ] fifty-cent coins.

The missing number in the box is _____.

[   ]

40. Each tennis ball weighs 65 g. Find the weight of the 5 marbles.

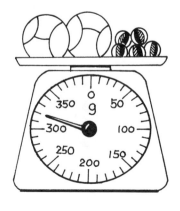

[   ] g

Section C (5 × 4 marks)

Work out the following sums in the space provided. Show all your working and steps clearly.

---

41. Mr Siva earns $45 a day.
    He earns 3 times as much as Mr Fu.
    How much money does Mr Fu earn a day?

    Answer: [＿＿＿＿]

---

42. I have a twenty-dollar note, 3 five-dollar notes, 3 twenty-cent coins and 3 five-cent coins.
    How much money do I have altogether?

    Answer: [＿＿＿＿]

---

43. Xiaoli weighs 42 kg. Xiaobao is 6 kg lighter.
    Their mother weighs twice as heavy as Xiaobao.
    What is their mother's weight?

    Answer: [＿＿＿＿]

---

44. Mrs Ravi bought a chopping board and a saucepan.
    Mrs Lee bought a wok.
    How much more did Mrs Lee spend than Mrs Ravi?

wok
$59.90

saucepan
$12.50

chopping board
$5.80

Answer:

45. At a sale, story books were sold at $3.90 each and magazines at 4 for $10.
    Jeremy bought 5 story books and 8 magazines.
    He gave the cashier a fifty-dollar note.
    How much change did he get back?

story books

$3.90 each

magazines

HOME   TEENAGE

4 for $10

Answer:

Capacity

1. How much water is shown in each container?

(a)
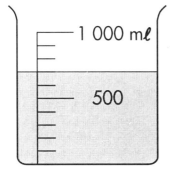

_____ mℓ

(b)
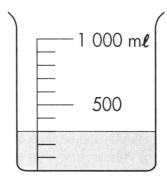

_____ mℓ

(c)
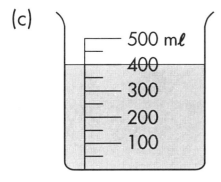

_____ mℓ

(d)
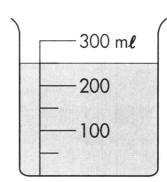

_____ mℓ

(e)
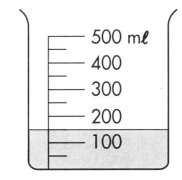

_____ mℓ

(f)

_____ mℓ

2. Write the missing numbers in the boxes.

(a) 560 ml + ☐ ml = 1 l

(b) 320 ml + ☐ ml = 1 l

(c) ☐ ml + 450 ml = 1 l

(d) 1 l − ☐ ml = 250 ml

(e) 1 l − ☐ ml = 300 ml

3. Match.

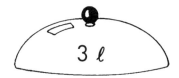

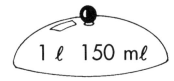

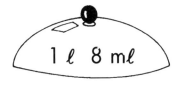

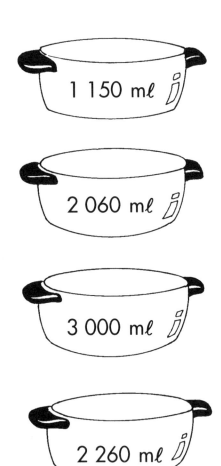

114

4. Fill in the blanks.

(a) 1 ℓ 200 mℓ = _____ mℓ

(b) 1 ℓ 755 mℓ = _____ mℓ

(c) 1 ℓ 56 mℓ = _____ mℓ

(d) 2 ℓ 80 mℓ = _____ mℓ

(e) 3 ℓ 6 mℓ = _____ mℓ

(f) 1 200 mℓ = _____ ℓ _____ mℓ

(g) 1 350 mℓ = _____ ℓ _____ mℓ

(h) 2 100 mℓ = _____ ℓ _____ mℓ

(i) 3 082 mℓ = _____ ℓ _____ mℓ

(j) 4 009 mℓ = _____ ℓ _____ mℓ

5. Write >, < or = in each ◯.

(a) 1 ℓ 450 mℓ ◯ 1 045 mℓ   (b) 1 ℓ ◯ 990 mℓ

(c) 2 ℓ 65 mℓ ◯ 2 065 mℓ   (d) 2 ℓ 5 mℓ ◯ 2 500 mℓ

(e) 3 ℓ 815 mℓ ◯ 3 850 mℓ   (f) 4 ℓ ◯ 4 000 mℓ

(g) 4 ℓ 20 mℓ ◯ 4 ℓ + 20 mℓ   (h) 4 ℓ 90 mℓ ◯ 5 ℓ − 10 mℓ

(i) 5 ℓ 125 mℓ ◯ 6 ℓ − 875 mℓ

(j) 5 ℓ 900 mℓ ◯ 6 ℓ − 10 mℓ

6. Complete the diagrams.

(a)

(b)

7. Do these sums.

(a)
```
     1 ℓ    500 mℓ
+            150 mℓ
─────────────────────
       ℓ         mℓ
─────────────────────
```

(b)
```
     2 ℓ    550 mℓ
+            450 mℓ
─────────────────────
       ℓ         mℓ
─────────────────────
```

(c)
```
     2 ℓ    400 mℓ
+            650 mℓ
─────────────────────
       ℓ         mℓ
─────────────────────
```

(d)
```
     3 ℓ    860 mℓ
+            440 mℓ
─────────────────────
       ℓ         mℓ
─────────────────────
```

(e)   2 ℓ   350 mℓ

    +   1 ℓ   455 mℓ

         ℓ   mℓ

(f)   3 ℓ   50 mℓ

    +   2 ℓ   868 mℓ

         ℓ   mℓ

(g)   3 ℓ   840 mℓ

    –   560 mℓ

         ℓ   mℓ

(h)   4 ℓ   740 mℓ

    –   880 mℓ

         ℓ   mℓ

(i)   3 ℓ   850 mℓ

    –   1 ℓ   975 mℓ

         ℓ   mℓ

(j)   5 ℓ   150 mℓ

    –   3 ℓ   380 mℓ

         ℓ   mℓ

8. Fill in the blanks based on the diagrams shown below.

 grape juice
330 mℓ

 milk
250 mℓ

 orange juice
250 mℓ

(a) The can of grape juice is _____ mℓ more than the packet of milk.

(b) The packet of _____ and the packet of _____ have the same capacity.

(c) Is the capacity of 2 packets of milk more or less than that of a can of grape juice?
It is _____ than a can of grape juice.

(d) The total capacity of the three items is _____ mℓ.

117

Do these sums carefully showing all your working and statements.

9. There are 330 mℓ of orange juice in a can.
   What is the total amount of orange juice in 6 cans?
   Give your answer in litres and millilitres.

   Answer: [＿＿＿] ℓ [＿＿＿] mℓ

10. Father bought 2 tins of engine oil.
    Each tin contained 3 ℓ of engine oil.
    After servicing his car, he had 2 ℓ 650 mℓ of oil left.
    How much oil did he use?

   Answer: [＿＿＿] ℓ [＿＿＿] mℓ

11. Mother made 5 litres of lime juice.
    She used 2 litres for making cocktail and poured the rest equally into 6 bottles.
    How much lime juice did she pour into 1 bottle?

    Answer: [＿＿＿＿] mℓ

---

12. A container holds $2\frac{1}{2}$ litres of water.

    1 litre of orange syrup is poured into the container to make orange juice. The orange juice is then served in glasses. If each glass can hold $\frac{1}{4}$ litre, how many such glasses are needed to contain all the orange juice?

    Answer: [＿＿＿＿]

13. Mother buys 1 carton of coke.
    Each carton contains 20 cans of coke.
    1 can of coke contains 250 ml of drinks.
    How many litres of drinks are there in 1 carton?

Answer: _____ ℓ

Graphs

1. The picture graph shows the capacities of 3 containers. Study it and fill in the blanks.

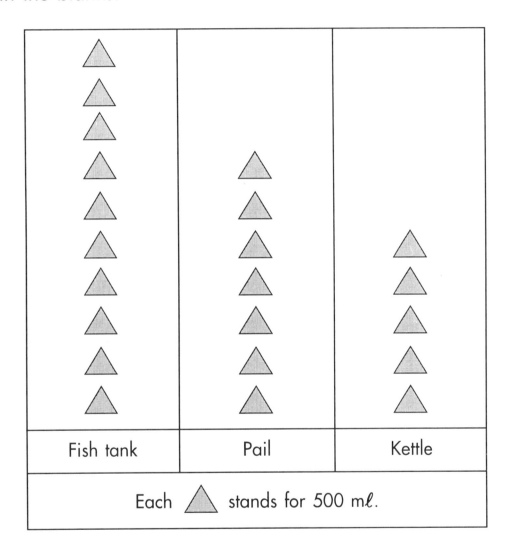

| Fish tank | Pail | Kettle |

Each △ stands for 500 mℓ.

(a) The capacity of the fish tank is _____ mℓ.

(b) The pail has a capacity of _____ mℓ.

(c) The _____ has the least capacity.

(d) The fish tank holds _____ mℓ of water more than the pail.

2. Study the graph. Then fill in the blanks.

Attendance At A School Library

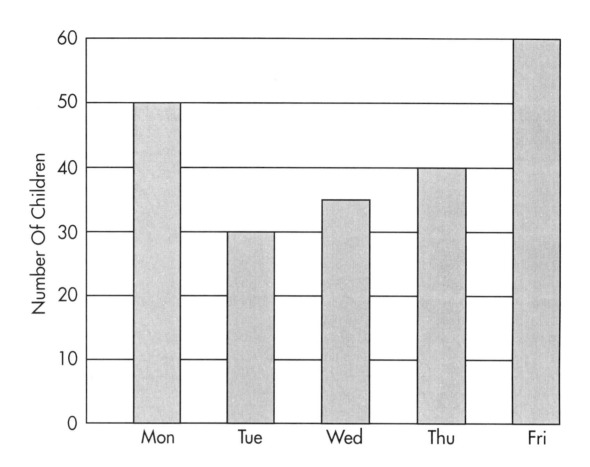

(a) _____ children visited the library on Thursday.

(b) The most number of children visited the library on _____.

(c) _____ more children visited the library on Monday than on Wednesday.

(d) The number of children who visited the library on Friday was twice the number who visited on _____.

(e) _____ children visited the library on Tuesday.

3. Study the graph. Then fill in the blanks.

Number Of Points Scored By 5 Teams

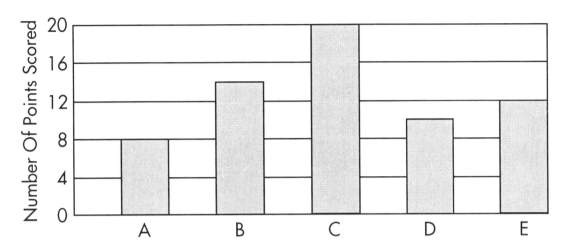

(a) Team _____ scored the least number of points.

(b) Team B scored _____ points.

(c) Team E scored _____ points less than Team C.

(d) Team _____ scored twice as many points as Team D.

(e) Team A and Team E scored _____ points altogether.

4. Study the graph. Then answer the questions.

Favourite Ice Cream Flavours Of Primary 3A

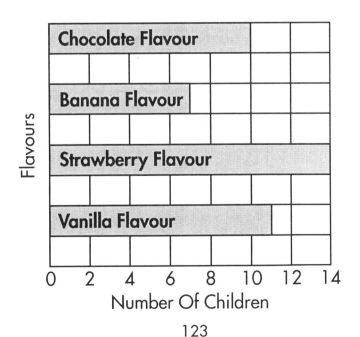

(a) How many children like vanilla flavour? _____

(b) How many more children like chocolate flavour than banana flavour? _____

(c) Which flavour do 14 children like? _____

(d) Which flavour is least liked by the children? _____

(e) How many children are there in the class? _____

5. Study the graph. Then answer the questions.

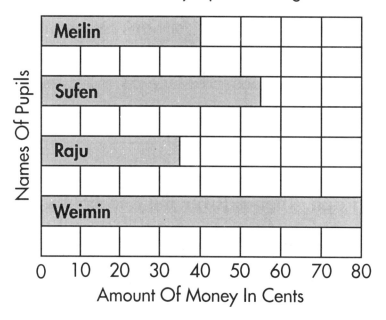

Amount Of Money Spent During Recess

(a) Who spent the least amount of money? _____

(b) How much did Sufen spend? _____

(c) Who spent half of what Weimin spend? _____

(d) How much more did Meilin spend than Raju? _____

(e) How much did the 4 children spend altogether? _____

CONTINUAL ASSESSMENT 2

Name: _____

Date: _____

 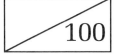

Time allowed: 1 h 30 min

Section A (20 × 2 marks)

Choose the correct answer and write its number in the brackets provided.

1. Which one of the following is equal to 107?
   (1) 50 + 47   (2) 20 + 87
   (3) 37 + 80   (4) 60 + 57   (   )

2. Which one of the following numbers is 70 less than 450?
   (1) 520   (2) 420   (3) 390   (4) 380   (   )

3. Which one of the following **does not** have the same value as 2 400?
   (1) 4 × 600   (2) 40 × 60
   (3) 24 × 10   (4) 20 × 120   (   )

4. $1.50 is the same as _____.

   (1) ($1) (20¢) (20¢) (10¢) (5¢)

   (2) (50¢) (50¢) (50¢) (5¢)

   (3) ($1) (20¢) (10¢) (10¢) (10¢)

   (4) ($1) (20¢) (10¢) (10¢) (5¢) (1¢)   (   )

5. $5.70 = _____ cents
   (1) 57   (2) 70
   (3) 570   (4) 5 700   ( )

6. Four hundred and four dollars and four cents is the same as
   _____.
   (1) $404.40   (2) $404.04
   (3) $400.40   (4) $400.04   ( )

7. How many 20-cent coins can be exchanged for $5.00?
   (1) 250   (2) 50
   (3) 25   (4) 20   ( )

8. Which one of the following items is the cheapest?
   (1)   (2)

$3.20

$40.90

   (3)   (4)

$10.90

$24.50   ( )

9. My water bottle can hold about _____ mℓ of water.
   (1) 5 000   (2) 500
   (3) 50   (4) 5   ( )

10. How much water is there in the container?

   100 mℓ   (1) 7 000 mℓ
   80
                                   (2) 700 mℓ
   60
   40   (3) 70 mℓ
   20
                                   (4) 7 mℓ   ( )

126

11. 2 ℓ 60 mℓ = _____ mℓ
    (1) 260   (2) 2 066
    (3) 2 060   (4) 2 600   (   )

12. 2 kg 30 g is the same as _____.
    (1) 23 g   (2) 203 g
    (3) 2 030 g   (4) 2 300 g   (   )

13. How much more water is needed to fill the container shown?

    (1) 250 mℓ
    (2) 300 mℓ
    (3) 700 mℓ
    (4) 750 mℓ   (   )

14. contain 750 mℓ of lemonade.

    Then contain [   ] mℓ of lemonade.
         (1) 2 500
         (2) 2 250
         (3) 1 750
         (4) 1 125   (   )

15. Sumei bought 2 twenty-cent stamps from the post office.
    She gave the cashier a one-dollar note.
    How much change did Sumei receive?
    (1) $0.20   (2) $0.40
    (3) $0.60   (4) $0.80   (   )

16. Which one of the following is equal to 30 ten-dollar notes?
    (1) $30 000   (2) $3 000
    (3) $300   (4) $30   (   )

Study the graph below carefully and answer questions 17 to 19.

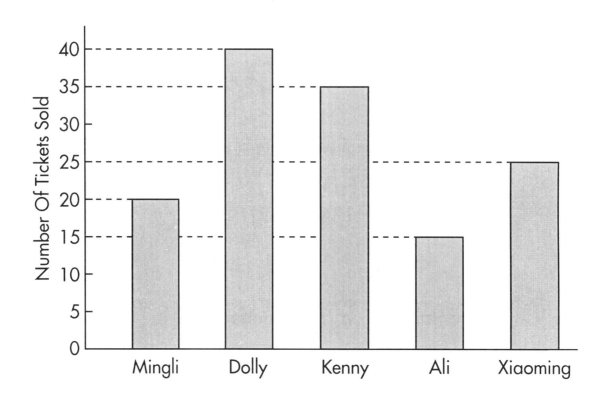

17. Kenny sold _____ more tickets than Mingli.
    (1) 10   (2) 15
    (3) 20   (4) 25   (   )

18. Ali and _____ sold 40 tickets altogether.
    (1) Xiaoming   (2) Kenny
    (3) Dolly   (4) Mingli   (   )

19. Ali sold _____ fewer tickets than Dolly.
    (1) 10   (2) 15
    (3) 20   (4) 25   (   )

20. Mr Jumat bought 5 tins of paint. Each tin contained 2 ℓ of paint.
    After painting his house, he had 2 ℓ 450 mℓ of paint left.
    How much paint did he use for painting his house?
    (1) 3 ℓ 450 mℓ   (2) 6 ℓ 550 mℓ
    (3) 7 ℓ 550 mℓ   (4) 8 ℓ 450 mℓ   ( )

Section B (20 × 2 marks)

Work out the answer for each question correctly. Write the answer in the box provided.

21. $20 − ☐ = $6.05.

    The missing value in the box is _____.   ☐

22. 705 mℓ + 1 ℓ 430 mℓ = _____ ℓ _____ mℓ

                                        ☐ ℓ ☐ mℓ

23. The value of 1 000 ÷ 8 is _____.   ☐

24. 240 tens ÷ 20 = _____   ☐

25. 6 hundreds × 9 = _____ tens   ☐

26. 5 ℓ 330 mℓ − 2 ℓ 900 mℓ = _____ ℓ _____ mℓ

                                        ☐ ℓ ☐ mℓ

The graph below shows the types of houses in which a group of Primary 3 children live.

Study it and then answer questions 27 to 29.

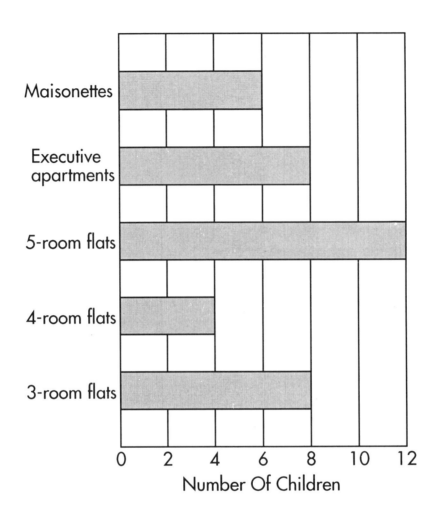

27. How many children live in 3-room flats?

28. (a) Do more children live in 5-room flats or executive apartments?
    (b) How many more?

    (a)

    (b)

29. How many children are there in the group?

30. Find the value of 400 − 186 − 14.

31. What is the value of 399 + 99 + 21?

32. Leela paid $4 for 10 erasers.
    How much did each eraser cost?

    $ ____

33. Each satay stick costs $0.30.
    What is the cost of 30 satay sticks?

    $ ____

34. Water from jug A and jug B is poured into an empty jug C.
    How much water is there in jug C now?

Jug A   Jug B   Jug C

____ mℓ

35. The capacity of a pail is 3 litres.
    There is 1 ℓ 480 mℓ of water in it.
    How much more water is needed to fill the pail?

    ____ ℓ ____ mℓ

36. A number has a quotient of 321 and a remainder of 2 when it is
    divided by 3. What is the number?

    ____

Study the diagrams below and answer questions 37 to 38.

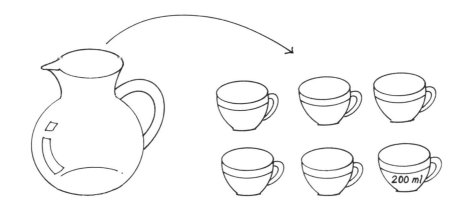

Each cup has the same capacity.

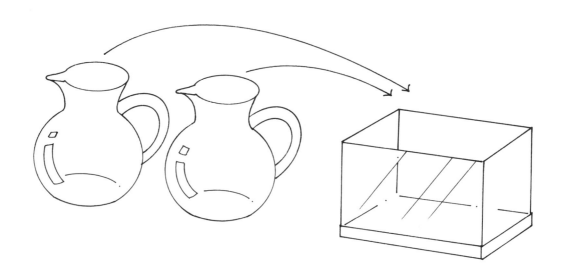

37. How many cups of water are needed to fill the tank? [ ]

38. What is the capacity of the tank? [ ] ℓ [ ] mℓ

39. Siti bought a story book which cost $11.10.
    It cost three times as much as a pen.
    How much would she need to pay for 2 pens? $ [ ]

40. Mother bought two 1-litre packets of milk.
    She drank 650 mℓ of it.
    How much milk was left? [ ] ℓ [ ] mℓ

Section C (5 × 4 marks)

Work out the following sums in the space provided. Show all your working and steps clearly.

---

41. Billy has 1 050 stamps.
    He has 284 fewer stamps than Jamil.
    How many stamps does Jamil have?

    Answer: [　　　]

---

42. Ali, Bala, Meiling and Jane had lunch together.
    The food cost $24 and the drinks cost $4.
    They shared the cost equally.
    How much did Jane pay?

    Answer: [　　　]

---

43. 3 588 concert tickets were sold on Friday.
    1 422 more concert tickets were sold on Saturday.
    How many concert tickets were sold on both days?

    Answer: [　　　]

---

44. Jason bought a pair of jeans for $25.90 and a T-shirt for $15.50.
He gave the cashier a fifty-dollar note.
How much change did he receive?

Answer:

45. Lionel, Rajiv and David shared a sum of $168.
Lionel's share was four times Rajiv's share.
David's share was twice Rajiv's share.
How much was David's share?

Answer:

Fractions

1. Complete the following.

(a) Draw lines to divide the set into 3 equal parts.

(b) Draw lines to divide the set into 4 equal parts.

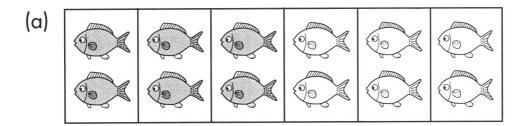

2. What fraction of the set is shaded?

(a)

_____

(b)

_____

3. (a) Which one of the pictures shows that $\frac{2}{3}$ of the rectangle is shaded?

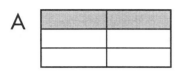 A

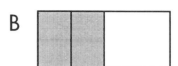 B

 C

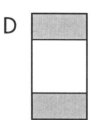 D

_____

(b) Which one of the pictures shows that $\frac{3}{4}$ of the circle is shaded?

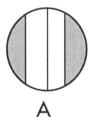 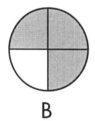 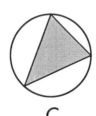 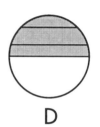

A   B   C   D   _____

4. What fraction of the figure is shaded?

(a)

_____

(b)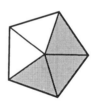

_____

(c)

_____

(d)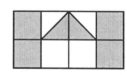

_____

(e)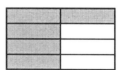

_____

(f)

_____

136

(g)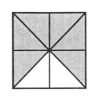

(h)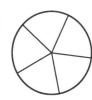

_____   _____

5. Colour each figure to show the given fraction.

(a)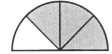

$\dfrac{2}{3}$

(b)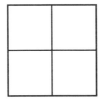

$\dfrac{3}{4}$

(c)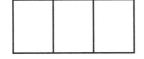

$\dfrac{2}{5}$

(d)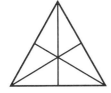

$\dfrac{5}{6}$

(e)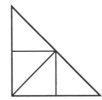

$\dfrac{1}{4}$

(f)

$\dfrac{1}{2}$

6. The bar is divided into 8 equal parts.

(a) $\dfrac{5}{8}$ of the bar is shaded.

$\dfrac{5}{8}$ is _____ out of the _____ equal parts.

(b) 1 whole = _____ eighths

$\dfrac{5}{8}$ = _____ eighths

(c) $\dfrac{5}{8}$ and _____ make 1 whole.

137

7. (a) Write down the denominator of the fraction $\frac{2}{7}$. _____

(b) Write down the numerator of the fraction $\frac{9}{10}$. _____

8. Ring the greatest fraction.

(a) $\frac{1}{12}, \frac{1}{10}, \frac{1}{7}$

(b) $\frac{1}{11}, \frac{1}{5}, \frac{1}{9}$

(c) $\frac{2}{13}, \frac{2}{6}, \frac{2}{9}$

(d) $\frac{8}{9}, \frac{8}{14}, \frac{8}{10}$

9. Ring the smallest fraction.

(a) $\frac{1}{3}, \frac{1}{8}, \frac{1}{2}$

(b) $\frac{1}{6}, \frac{1}{10}, \frac{1}{4}$

(c) $\frac{7}{8}, \frac{7}{10}, \frac{7}{14}$

(d) $\frac{4}{16}, \frac{4}{12}, \frac{4}{9}$

10. Arrange the fractions in order, beginning with the smallest.

(a) $\frac{1}{10}, \frac{1}{4}, \frac{1}{6}$ _____

(b) $\frac{2}{3}, \frac{2}{9}, \frac{2}{7}$ _____

11. Arrange the fractions in order, beginning with the greatest.

(a) $\frac{1}{5}, \frac{1}{8}, \frac{1}{6}$ _____

(b) $\frac{4}{12}, \frac{4}{9}, \frac{4}{14}$ _____

12. Write the missing numbers.

(a)

$\dfrac{3}{9}$ $\dfrac{4}{9}$

(b)
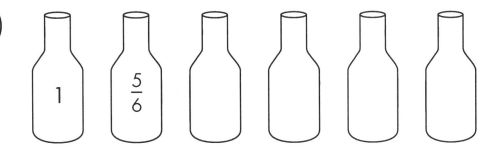

1 $\dfrac{5}{6}$

13. Write > or < in each ◯.

(a)
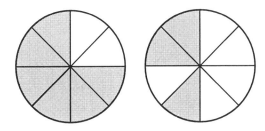

$\dfrac{6}{8}$ ◯ $\dfrac{3}{8}$

(b)
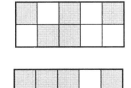

$\dfrac{5}{10}$ ◯ $\dfrac{8}{10}$

14. Write the missing numerators or denominators.

(a) $\dfrac{1}{4} = \dfrac{}{8}$

(b) $\dfrac{2}{6} = \dfrac{1}{}$

(c) $\dfrac{4}{5} = \dfrac{8}{}$

(d) $\dfrac{1}{2} = \dfrac{}{10}$

(e) $1 = \dfrac{}{9} = \dfrac{4}{}$

(f) $\dfrac{8}{16} = \dfrac{}{8} = \dfrac{1}{}$

15. Ring the equivalent fraction for each of the given fractions.

(a) 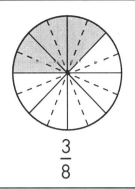 $\frac{3}{8}$	$\frac{3}{4},\quad \frac{6}{16},\quad \frac{1}{2}$
(b) 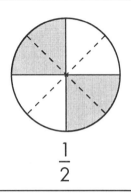 $\frac{1}{2}$	$\frac{4}{8},\quad \frac{4}{5},\quad \frac{8}{9}$
(c) 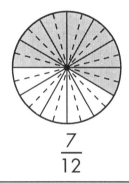 $\frac{7}{12}$	$\frac{4}{8},\quad \frac{9}{10},\quad \frac{14}{24}$
(d) 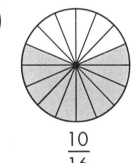 $\frac{10}{16}$	$\frac{2}{3},\quad \frac{5}{8},\quad \frac{7}{9}$

16. Write > or < in each $\bigcirc$.

(a) $\frac{5}{8} \bigcirc \frac{3}{4}$

(b) $\frac{2}{3} \bigcirc \frac{2}{5}$

(c) $\frac{8}{12} \bigcirc \frac{9}{9}$

(d) $\frac{6}{10} \bigcirc \frac{3}{6}$

17. Arrange the fractions in order, beginning with the smallest.

(a) $\frac{3}{5}$, $\frac{4}{6}$, $\frac{1}{2}$ _____

(b) $\frac{1}{3}$, $\frac{1}{8}$, $\frac{2}{10}$ _____

18. Add.

(a) $\frac{1}{4} + \frac{3}{4} = \Box$

(b) $\frac{6}{10} + \frac{1}{10} = \Box$

(c) $\frac{1}{2} + 1 = \Box$

(d) $\frac{1}{5} + \frac{3}{5} = \Box$

(e) $\frac{2}{12} + \frac{4}{12} + \frac{6}{12} = \Box$

(f) $\frac{1}{10} + \frac{5}{10} + \frac{8}{10} = \Box$

(g) $\frac{3}{8} + \frac{2}{4} = \Box$

(h) $\frac{1}{3} + \frac{5}{6} = \Box$

(i) $\frac{2}{10} + \frac{4}{5} = \Box$

(j) $\frac{1}{2} + \frac{3}{6} = \Box$

19. Subtract.

(a) $\frac{1}{2} - \frac{1}{2} = \Box$

(b) $\frac{7}{8} - \frac{5}{8} = \Box$

(c) $1 - \frac{7}{10} = \Box$

(d) $\frac{5}{9} - \frac{3}{9} = \Box$

(e) $\frac{6}{8} - \frac{2}{8} - \frac{1}{8} = \Box$

(f) $\frac{10}{12} - \frac{6}{12} - \frac{3}{12} = \Box$

(g) $\dfrac{5}{6} - \dfrac{1}{3} = $ ☐

(h) $\dfrac{2}{3} - \dfrac{1}{6} = $ ☐

(i) $\dfrac{1}{2} - \dfrac{2}{6} = $ ☐

(j) $\dfrac{3}{4} - \dfrac{1}{12} = $ ☐

Do these sums carefully showing all your working and statements.

20. Mary had a cake. She cut it into 3 equal pieces. She ate 1 piece. What fraction of the cake was left?

Answer: ☐

21. Rose was given $\dfrac{1}{2}$ a cake. She ate $\dfrac{1}{2}$ of it.
What fraction of the cake was left?

Answer: ☐

22. Liza had 12 flowers. She gave away $\frac{1}{4}$ of them.

How many flowers had she left?

Answer: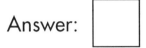

23. I have $10. I spend $\frac{1}{2}$ of it.

How much money have I left?

Answer: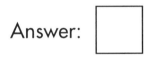

24. Mother bought $\frac{3}{4}$ m of ribbon. She used $\frac{1}{2}$ m.

How much ribbon had she left?

Answer:

Time

1. Draw lines to match the correct time.

7.15

8.25

9.52

1.03

2.38

4.26

5.39

6.17

2. Write the correct time in each blank.

(a)

_____

(b)

_____

(c)

_____

(d)

_____

(e)

_____

(f)

_____

3. Draw the hour hand and the minute hand to show the given time.

(a)

3.52

(b)

6.23

(c)
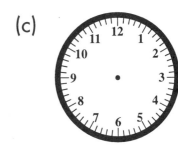

8.47

(d)

4.09

(e)

7.30

(f)
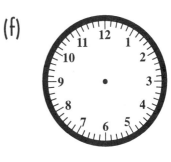

11.06

145

4. Complete the following.

(a)

| 6.30 | 7.15 |

_____ minutes later

(b)

| 2.40 | 4.40 |

_____ hours later

(c)

| 8.15 | 11.50 |

_____ h _____ min later

5. Write in hours and minutes.

   (a) 1 h 20 min = _____ min

   (b) 100 min = _____ h _____ min

   (c) 2 h = _____ min

   (d) 60 min = _____ h _____ min

   (e) 1 h 30 min = _____ min

   (f) 140 min = _____ h _____ min

   (g) 2 h 40 min = _____ min

   (h) 200 min = _____ h _____ min

   (i) 3 h 10 min = _____ min

   (j) 86 min = _____ h _____ min

   (k) 3 h 25 min = _____ min

   (l) 135 min = _____ h _____ min

6. Add.

   (a)   42 min
         +   18 min
         _____
                   min = _____ h _____ min
         _____

   (b)   53 min
         +   34 min
         _____
                   min = _____ h _____ min
         _____

(c)   48 min
    +   29 min

          min = _____ h _____ min

(d)   39 min
    +   24 min

          min = _____ h _____ min

(e)   45 min
    +   45 min

          min = _____ h _____ min

(f)   23 min
    +   57 min

          min = _____ h _____ min

7. Subtract.

(a)   90 min
    −   24 min

          min = _____ h _____ min

(b)   80 min
    −   13 min

          min = _____ h _____ min

(c)   76 min
    −   6 min

          min = _____ h _____ min

(d)   100 min
    −   36 min
    ─────────────
          min   = _____ h _____ min
    ─────────────

(e)   102 min
    −   26 min
    ─────────────
          min   = _____ h _____ min
    ─────────────

(f)   114 min
    −   52 min
    ─────────────
          min   = _____ h _____ min
    ─────────────

8. Write the missing numbers.

(a) 10 seconds + ⬜ seconds = 1 minute

(b) 28 seconds + ⬜ seconds = 1 minute

(c) 1 minute − ⬜ seconds = 18 seconds

(d) 1 minute − ⬜ seconds = 24 seconds

(e) 3 minutes = ⬜ seconds

(f) 225 seconds = ⬜ minutes ⬜ seconds

149

9. Match.

2 years 3 months ○	○ 53 months
3 years 8 months ○	○ 16 months
1 year 4 months ○	○ 36 months
4 years 5 months ○	○ 27 months
3 years ○	○ 44 months

10. Write in years and months.

(a) 28 months = _____ years _____ months

(b) 47 months = _____ years _____ months

(c) 18 months = _____ year _____ months

(d) 50 months = _____ years _____ months

11. Write in days.

    (a) 3 weeks 4 days = _____ days

    (b) 1 week 6 days = _____ days

    (c) 5 weeks 2 days = _____ days

    (d) 4 weeks 5 days = _____ days

12. Write in weeks and days.

    (a) 15 days = _____ weeks _____ day(s)

    (b) 29 days = _____ weeks _____ day(s)

    (c) 38 days = _____ weeks _____ day(s)

    (d) 64 days = _____ weeks _____ day(s)

Do these sums carefully showing all your working and statements.

13. Meili practised on her piano for 35 min on Monday and 40 min on Tuesday.
    How much time did she spend practising on her piano on the 2 days?

Answer: ⬚ min

151

14. John took 45 min to do a test.
    Raju took 50 min to do the same test.
    How much faster was John?

    Answer: [   ] min

15. Minghao took 40 min to cycle to the swimming pool and 45 min to cycle home.
    How much time did he spend cycling altogether?

    Answer: [   ] h [   ] min

16. Paul took 55 min to read a comic book.
    Shihui took 8 min less to read the same book.
    How much time did Shihui take to read the book?

    Answer: [   ] min

REVISION 4

Name: _____

Date: _____

Marks: / 100

Time allowed: 1 h 30 min

Section A (20 × 2 marks)

Choose the correct answer and write its number in the brackets provided.

1. The value of 2 in 3 241 is _____.
   - (1) 2
   - (2) 20
   - (3) 200
   - (4) 2 000   (   )

2. In 1 505, [____], 1 545, 1 565, 1 585, the missing number in the number pattern is _____.
   - (1) 1 510
   - (2) 1 515
   - (3) 1 520
   - (4) 1 525   (   )

3. The number that is 100 less than 610 is _____.
   - (1) 500
   - (2) 510
   - (3) 600
   - (4) 710   (   )

4. 655 × 0 = _____
   - (1) 6 550
   - (2) 6 505
   - (3) 655
   - (4) 0   (   )

5. Which one of the following can be divided by 3 exactly?
   - (1) 211
   - (2) 323
   - (3) 324
   - (4) 401   (   )

6. What fraction of the figure is shaded?

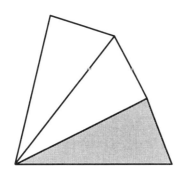

(1) $\frac{2}{3}$

(2) $\frac{1}{2}$

(3) $\frac{1}{3}$

(4) $\frac{1}{4}$

(   )

7. The value of $\frac{3}{8} + \frac{1}{8}$ is _____.

(1) $\frac{4}{8}$ (2) $\frac{2}{8}$ (3) $\frac{4}{16}$ (4) $\frac{3}{16}$ (   )

8. $\frac{4}{5} - \boxed{} = \frac{1}{5}$.

The missing number in the box is _____.

(1) 1   (2) $\frac{3}{5}$ (3) $\frac{2}{5}$ (4) $\frac{1}{5}$ (   )

9. In the figure below, what is the missing number in the box?

	1		
	$\frac{1}{2}$		
$\frac{7}{8}$ $\frac{3}{8}$		$\frac{1}{3}$ $\frac{5}{6}$	
	$\frac{1}{5}$		
	$\frac{7}{10}$		

(1) 1   (2) $\frac{3}{4}$

(3) $\frac{1}{2}$ (4) $\frac{4}{6}$ (   )

10. Which one of the following shows a quarter to 3?

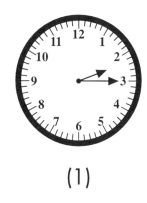

(1)

(2)

(3)

(4)   (   )

11. The denominator of $\frac{4}{9}$ is _____.

    (1) 13   (2) 9   (3) 5   (4) 4   (   )

12. Which one of the following gives the largest value?

    (1) $\frac{1}{8} + \frac{3}{8}$ (2) $1 - \frac{1}{8}$

    (3) $\frac{2}{8} + \frac{3}{8}$ (4) $\frac{7}{8} - \frac{2}{8}$ (   )

13. 210 cents is the same as _____.
    (1) $0.21   (2) $2.10
    (3) $21.00   (4) $210.00   (   )

14. $\boxed{} \div 5 = 30$ cents.

    The missing value in the box is _____.
    (1) $150   (2) $15   (3) $1.50   (4) $0.15 (   )

15. 6 years 5 months is the same as _____ months.
    (1) 77   (2) 65   (3) 11   (4) 6   (   )

16. How much water is there in the container?

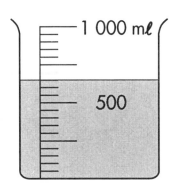

(1) 550 mℓ

(2) 650 mℓ

(3) 750 mℓ

(4) 850 mℓ   (   )

Study the graph below carefully and then answer questions 17 to 19.

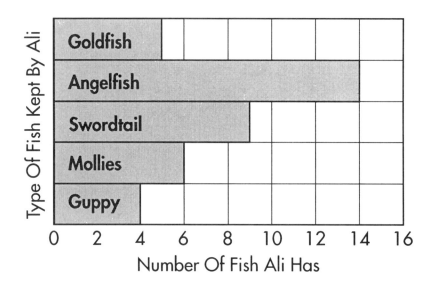

17. How many swordtails does Ali have?
    (1) 6   (2) 8   (3) 9   (4) 14   (   )

18. How many more angelfish than swordtails has he?
    (1) 5   (2) 9   (3) 14   (4) 23   (   )

19. How many fish has Ali altogether?
    (1) 38   (2) 34   (3) 28   (4) 14   (   )

20. Sally has three 50-cent coins and four 20-cent coins. She has _____ altogether.
    (1) $0.70   (2) $1.50   (3) $2.30   (4) $2.50 (   )

Section B (20 × 2 marks)

Write your answers in the boxes provided.

21. The value of 1 809 + 291 is _____.

22. $24.60 ÷ 4 = _____ $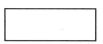

23. $1\frac{1}{2}$ hours is the same as _____ minutes.

24. Mr Lin weighs 62 500 g. His wife weighs 18 kg less.
    What is the weight of his wife?   ☐ kg ☐ g

25. Ali watches a television programme from 6.30 p.m. to 7.15 p.m.
    How long does the programme last?    min

26. A container can hold 3 ℓ 175 mℓ of water.
    A bottle can hold 1 ℓ 600 mℓ of water.
    How much more water can the container hold than the bottle?
     mℓ

27. Shade $\frac{2}{5}$ of the figure shown.

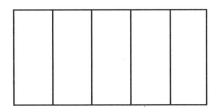

28. $\frac{3}{4} +$ ☐ $= \frac{10}{12}$

    What is the missing value in the box?

29. 4 kg 23 g = _____ g

30. 3 weeks 5 days = _____ days

31. Alvin started to do his homework at 11.30 a.m. and finished it at 1.05 p.m. How many hours and minutes did he take?

    [ ] h [ ] min

32. The clock shown below is 15 minutes fast.
    What should be the correct time?

33. A tin of biscuits weighs 2 kg 250 g. What is the weight of 3 such tins of biscuits?

    [ ] kg [ ] g

34.

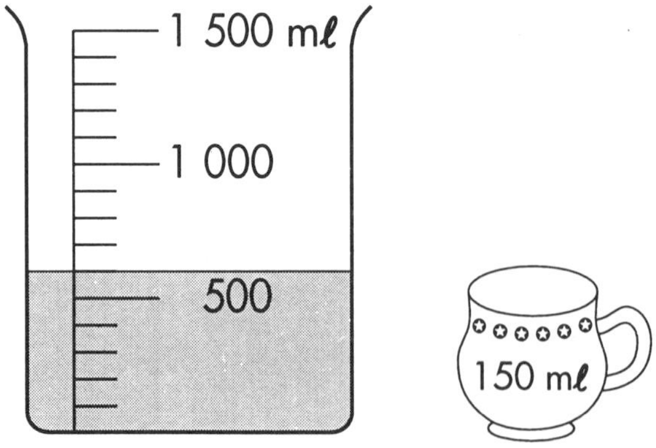

Each cup can contain 150 mℓ of water.

Study the diagram above carefully. There is some water in the container. How many cups of water are needed to fill the container to 1 500 mℓ?

35. It is 8.00 a.m. now. 5 h 10 min later, it will be _____ p.m.

36. Mrs Wu paid $1 029 for some flower pots. If each flower pot cost $7, how many of them did she buy?

37. A rope is 2 m 40 cm long.
    Another rope is 3 m 80 cm long.
    What is the total length of the two ropes.

    [ ] m [ ] cm

38. Find the value of $\frac{6}{7} - \frac{1}{7} - \frac{4}{7}$.

39. $\star + \triangle = 30$

    $\triangle + \bigcirc = 12$

    $\star + \triangle + \triangle + \bigcirc = ?$

40. Jeremy thought of a number.
    He multiplied it by 6 and then subtracted 4 from the result.
    His answer was 38.
    What was the number that Jeremy first thought of?

Section C (5 × 4 marks)

Work out the following sums in the space provided. Show all your working and steps carefully.

41. There were 2 280 pupils in a school.
1 496 of them were boys.
How many of them were girls?

Answer:

42. A running track is 600 m long.
Peihua ran round the track 5 times.
Bala ran 500 m more than Peihua.
What was the distance covered by Bala?

Answer: ____ m

43. Melvin has a packet of balloons. $\frac{2}{5}$ of the balloons are red, $\frac{7}{15}$ of them are green and the rest are yellow.
What fraction of the balloons are yellow?

Answer: [ ]

---

44. Faisal took 25 minutes to go to school.
He reached school at 7.05 a.m.
When did he leave his house?

Answer: [ ]

---

45. Mr Gopi bought a durian and a papaya for $10.
The durian cost 3 times as much as the papaya.
How much would he have to pay for two durians and a papaya?

Answer: $ [ ]

EXERCISE 14

Geometry

1. Mark the angles of each figure. Then complete the table below.

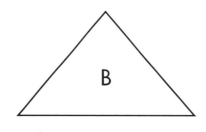

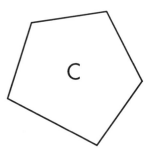

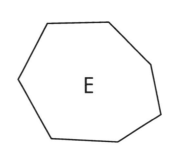

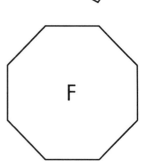

Figure	Number of sides	Number of angles
A		
B		
C		
D		
E		
F		

2. Look at the following figures carefully. Then complete the table below. The first one has been done for you. You may use a piece of paper to help you.

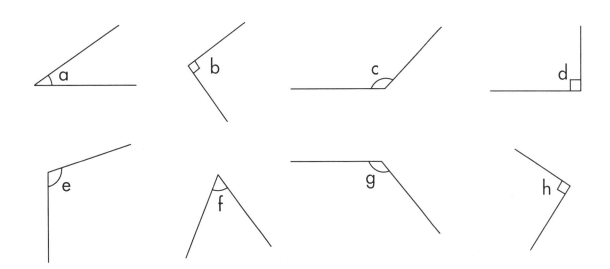

Smaller than a right angle	Equal to a right angle	Bigger than a right angle
a		

3. Fill in the blanks.

(a)

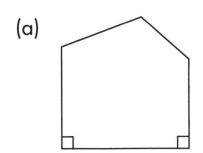

There are _____ angles inside the figure.

There are _____ right angles.

(b)

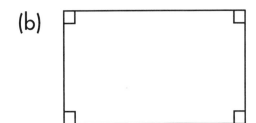

There are _____ angles inside the rectangle.

There are _____ right angles in a rectangle.

(c)

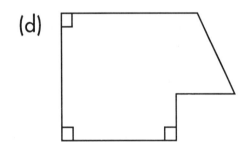

There are _____ angles inside this figure.

There is _____ right angle.

(d)

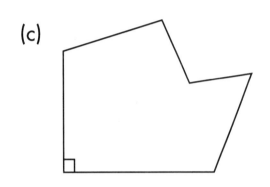

There are _____ angles inside this figure.

There are _____ right angles.

(e)

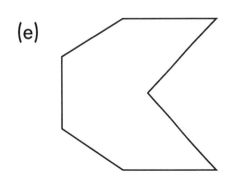

There are _____ angles inside this figure.

There are _____ right angles.

(f)

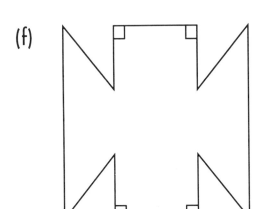

There are _____ angles inside this figure.

There are _____ right angles.

(g)

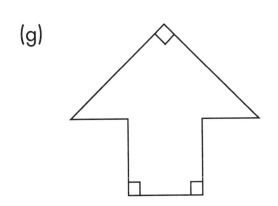

There are _____ angles inside this figure.

There are _____ right angles.

Area And Perimeter

1. Colour the area of each figure in red.

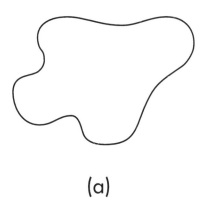

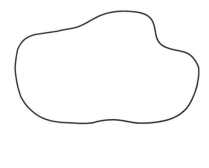

(a)

(b)

2. Go over the perimeter of each figure in blue.

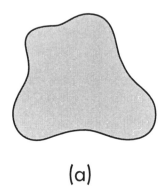

(a)

(b)

3. Use a ruler to measure the perimeter of each figure.

(a)

The perimeter is about _____ cm.

(b)

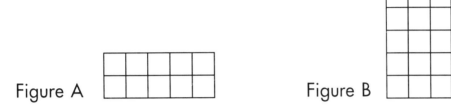

The perimeter is about _____ cm.

(c) Which figure has a longer perimeter?

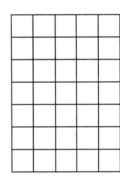

Figure A   Figure B

Figure _____ has a longer perimeter.

(d) Which figure has a smaller area?

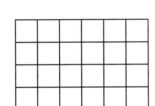

Figure A   Figure B

Figure _____ has a smaller area.

4. Find the area of each figure.

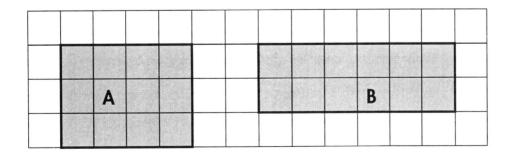

(a) Area of A = _____ square units.

(b) Area of B = _____ square units.

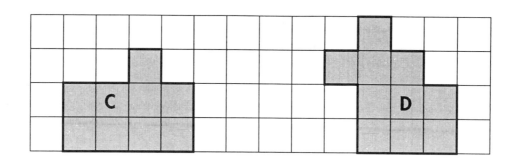

(c) Area of C = _____ square units.

(d) Area of D = _____ square units.

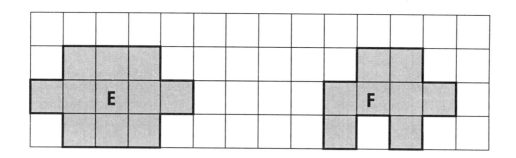

(e) Area of E = _____ square units.

(f) Area of F = _____ square units.

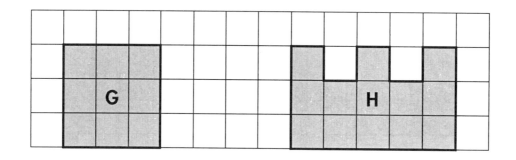

(g) Area of G = _____ square units.

(h) Area of H = _____ square units.

5. Find the area of each shape by counting the squares and triangles.

(a)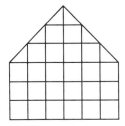

Area = _____ square units.

(b)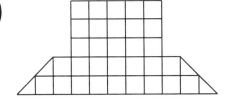

Area = _____ square units.

(c)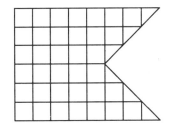

Area = _____ square units.

(d)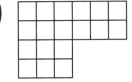

Area = _____ square units.

(e)

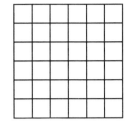

Area = _____ square units.

(f)

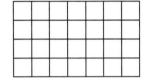

Area = _____ square units.

(g)

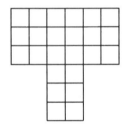

Area = _____ square units.

(h)

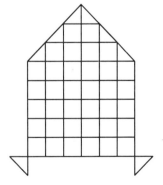

Area = _____ square units.

6. Fill in the blanks.

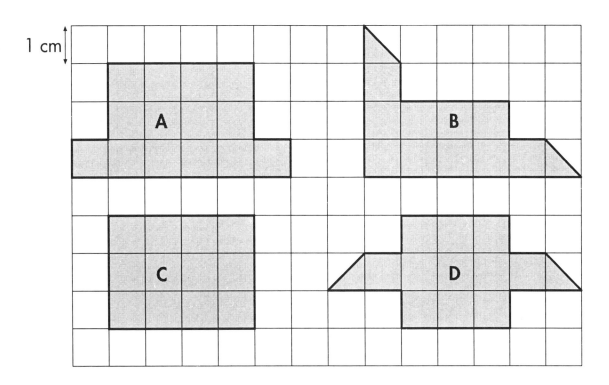

(a) Figure _____ has the smallest area.

(b) The area of figure _____ is equal to 11 cm².

(c) Figure C and figure _____ have the same area.

7. Fill in the blanks.

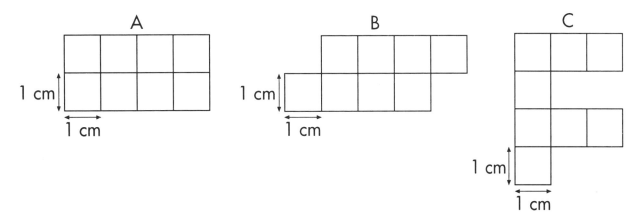

(a) The perimeter of figure _____ is 14 cm.

(b) Figure A has a perimeter of _____ cm.

(c) Figure _____ has the longest perimeter.

171

8. Find the perimeter of the following figures.

(a)

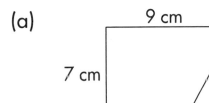

Answer: _____ cm

(b)

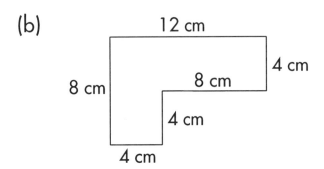

Answer: _____ cm

(c)

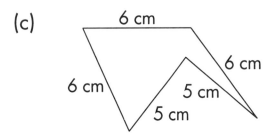

Answer: _____ cm

9. Find the area of each rectangle.

(a)

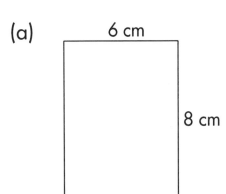

Answer: _____ cm^2

(b)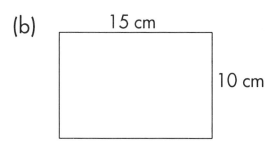

Answer: _____ cm²

(c)

20 cm

8 cm

Answer: _____ cm²

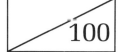

Name: _____   Marks:

Date: _____

Time allowed: 1 h 30 min

Section A (20 × 2 marks)

Choose the correct answer and write its number in the brackets provided.

1. 9 401 is the same as _____.
    (1) 9 000 + 4 + 1
    (2) 9 000 + 40 + 1
    (3) 9 000 + 400 + 1
    (4) 9 000 + 400 + 10   ( )

2. How many hundreds are there in 7 700?
    (1) 7   (2) 77
    (3) 700   (4) 770   ( )

3. 8 × ☐ = 24 × 4.

    The missing number in the box is _____.
    (1) 12   (2) 14
    (3) 88   (4) 104   ( )

4. Which one of the following has a different value from the rest?
    (1) 16 × 100   (2) 4 × 400
    (3) 40 × 40   (4) 100 × 40   ( )

5. Which one of the following has the **largest** value?
    (1) 400 ÷ 4   (2) 5 400 ÷ 6
    (3) 1 000 ÷ 10   (4) 720 ÷ 8   ( )

174

6. Which one of the following is the **longest**?

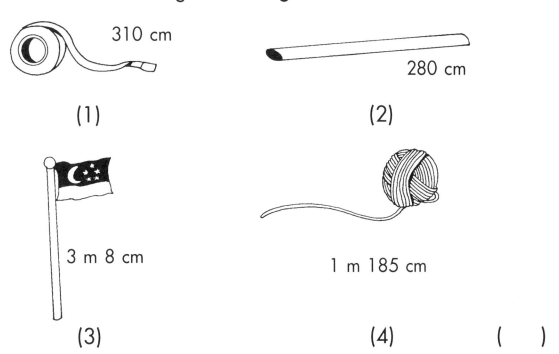

310 cm

280 cm

(1)

(2)

3 m 8 cm

1 m 185 cm

(3)

(4)

( )

7. What is the weight of the chicken?

(1) 2 g
(2) 20 g
(3) 200 g
(4) 2 000 g

( )

8. How many 20-cent coins can you get for a ten-dollar note?
(1) 10   (2) 20   (3) 50   (4) 100   ( )

9. Norlina has five 50-cent coins and six 20-cent coins.
She has _____ altogether.
(1) $3.70   (2) $2.50   (3) $1.20   (4) $0.70   ( )

10. How much water is needed to fill the container shown?

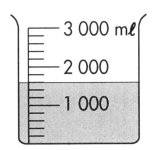

3 000 mℓ

2 000

1 000

(1) 1 600 mℓ
(2) 1 ℓ 500 mℓ
(3) 1 ℓ 400 mℓ
(4) 1 080 mℓ

( )

11. What fraction of the circle is shaded?

(1) $\frac{2}{5}$ (2) $\frac{3}{5}$

(3) $\frac{2}{3}$ (4) $\frac{3}{4}$

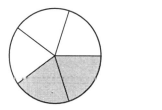

(   )

12. Which one of the following is **not** equal to $\frac{2}{3}$?

(1) $\frac{6}{9}$ (2) $\frac{8}{12}$ (3) $\frac{4}{6}$ (4) $\frac{12}{15}$ (   )

13. What fraction of the figure shown is **not** shaded?

(1) $\frac{1}{4}$ (2) $\frac{2}{4}$

(3) $\frac{2}{6}$ (4) $\frac{6}{8}$

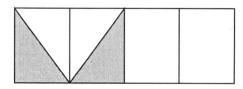

(   )

14. Find the value of $\frac{1}{7} + \frac{2}{7} + \frac{3}{7}$.

(1) $\frac{7}{7}$ (2) $\frac{6}{7}$ (3) $\frac{5}{7}$ (4) $\frac{4}{7}$ (   )

15. Fandi took 40 minutes to do his homework.
If he finished at 7.10 p.m., at what time did he start?

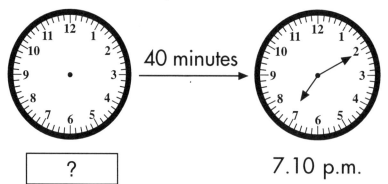

(1) 7.50 a.m.   (2) 7.50 p.m.
(3) 6.30 a.m.   (4) 6.30 p.m.   (   )

16. 210 seconds is the same as _____.
(1) 2 min 10 s   (2) 2 min 30 s
(3) 3 min 18 s   (4) 3 min 30 s   (   )

17. The figure shown has _____ right angles.

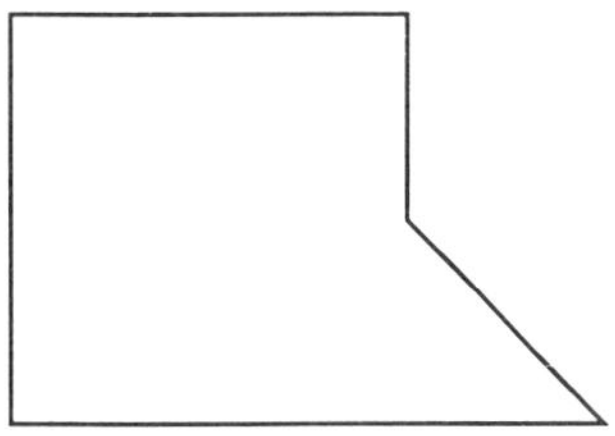

    (1) 1
    (2) 2
    (3) 3
    (4) 4   (   )

18. The area of triangle A is _____ cm^2 more than that of triangle B.

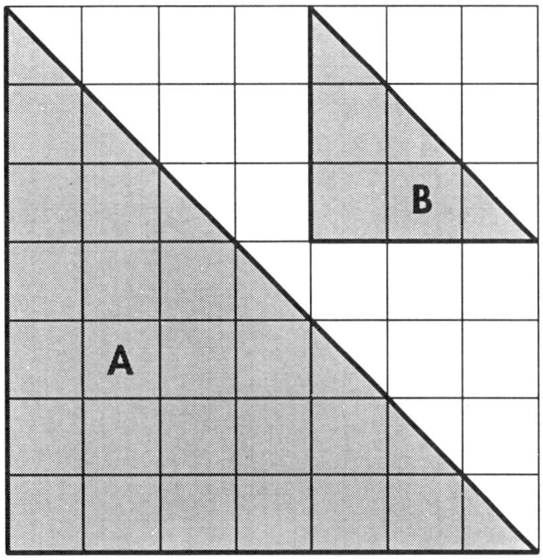

    (1) 29

    (2) 25

    (3) 23

    (4) 20   (   )

19. Which one of the following figures does **not** have the same area as the rest?

    (1)
    8 cm
    6 cm

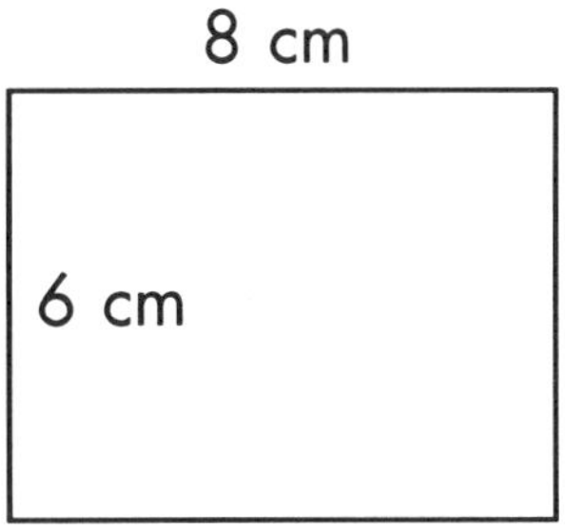

    (2)
    18 cm
    2 cm

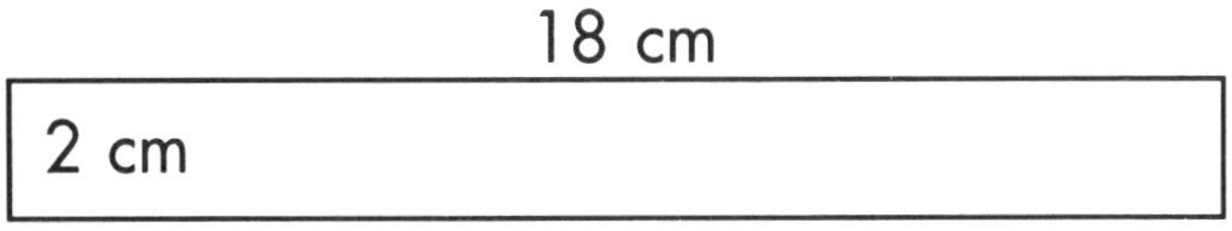

    (3) 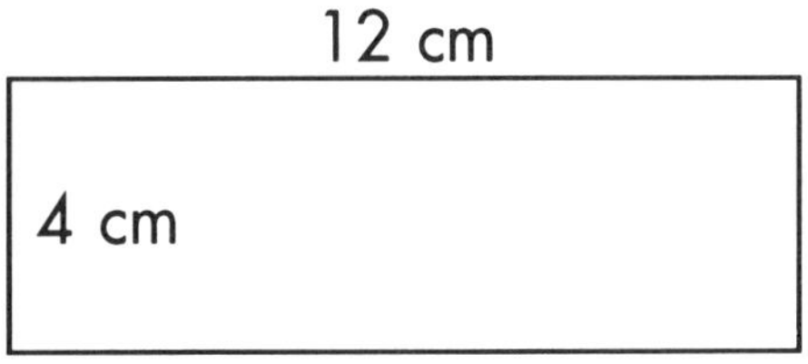
    12 cm
    4 cm

    (4)
    24 cm
    2 cm   (   )

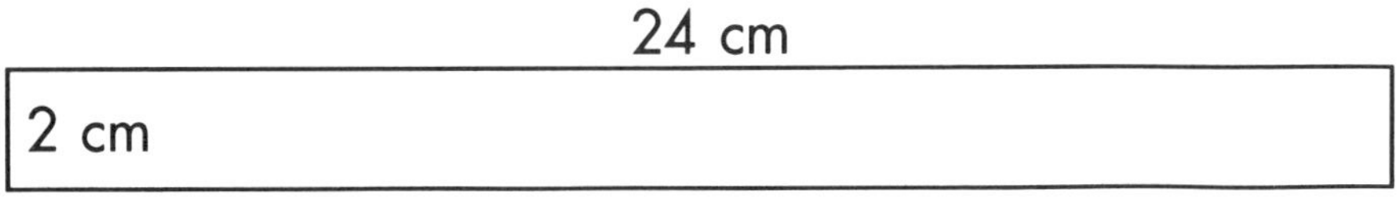

20. The figures are made up of 1-cm squares.
    Which two of the figures have the same perimeter?

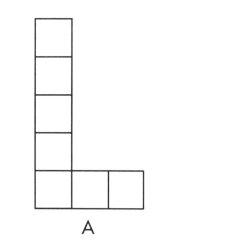

A

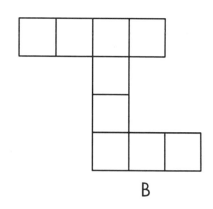

B

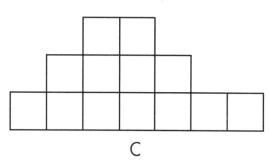

C

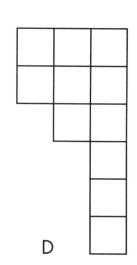

D

(1) A and B
(3) B and C

(2) A and D
(4) C and D   (   )

Section B (20 × 2 marks)

Work out the answer for each question and write it in the box provided.

21. $\boxed{}$ − 213 = 447.

    The missing number in the box is _____.

22. Divide 149 by 3. The remainder is _____.

23.   408
     ×   7
     _____
     [   ]   [   ]

24. Study the diagram below carefully.

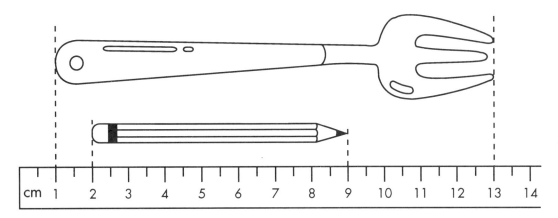

The fork is _____ cm longer than the pencil.   [   ]

25.

Each marble weighs 42 g.
What is the weight of the 2 tennis balls?   [   ] g

26. The value of 408 – 18 – 12 is _____.   [   ]

27. 4 mangoes cost $9.00.
How much does one mango cost?   [   ]

28. Study the diagrams carefully.

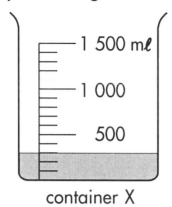

container X

Each cup can contain 100 mℓ of water.

There is some water in container X.
How many 100-mℓ cups of water do I need to fill container X to 1 500 mℓ?

29. 7 wholes = [ ] quarters.

The missing number in the box is _____.

30. $\frac{11}{12}$ = [ ] + $\frac{3}{4}$.

What is the missing fraction in the box?

31. Find the value of $\frac{7}{8} - \frac{1}{4}$.

32.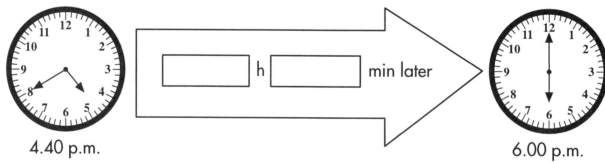

4.40 p.m.

[ ] h [ ] min later

6.00 p.m.

What are the missing numbers in the boxes?

[ ] h [ ] min

33. 58 months = _____ years _____ months

　　　　　　　　　　　　　[　　　　] years [　　　　] months

34. How many angles are there inside the figure below?

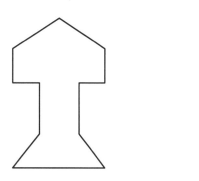

　　　　　　　　　　　　　　　　　　　　　　[　　　　]

35. The area of a square with side 9 cm is _____.

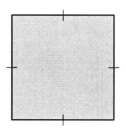

　　　　　　　　　　　　　　　　　　　[　　　　] cm²

36. The square and the rectangle shown below have the same perimeter. What is the length of one side of the square?

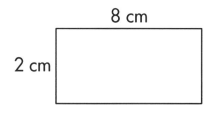 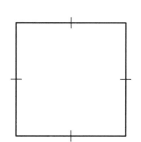

　　　　　　　　　　　　　　　　　　　[　　　　] cm

37. ◯ + △ = 14

　　◯ + ◯ = 12

　　△ + △ + △ = [　　　　]

　　The missing number in the box is _____.　　[　　　　]

181

The graph below shows the number of computer games sold by Mr Byte. Study the graph carefully and answer questions 38 to 40.

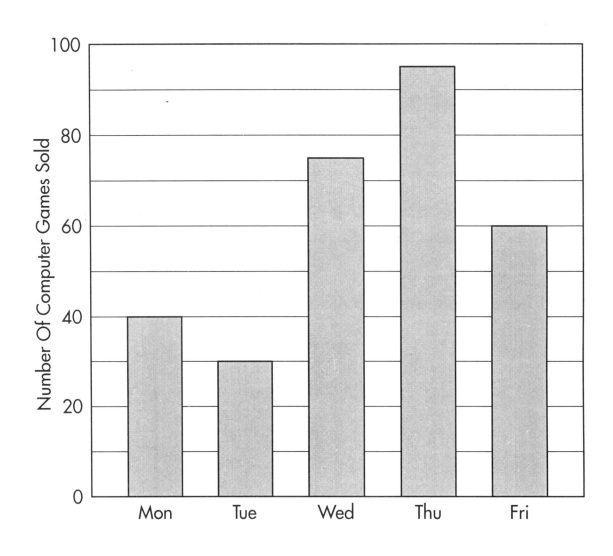

38. On which day did Mr Byte sell twice as many computer games as on Tuesday?

39. The number of computer games sold on Thursday is _____ more than that sold on Wednesday.

40. Find the total number of computer games sold on the five days.

Section C (5 × 4 marks)

Work out the following sums in the space provided. Show all your working and steps clearly.

41. David has 114 stamps and Andy has 2 500 stamps.
    How many more stamps does Andy have than David?

Answer: [ ]

42. Betty has a packet of beads.
    $\frac{1}{5}$ of them are red, $\frac{8}{15}$ of them are green and the rest are blue.
    What fraction of the beads are blue?

Answer: [ ]

43. 2 parcels, P and Q, weigh 5 kg 40 g altogether.
    Parcel P weighs 34 g less than parcel Q.
    What is the weight of parcel Q in kilograms and grams?

Answer: ☐ kg ☐ g

44. Mrs Wu bought 120 mangoes. She put them into two packets, A and B. Packet A had 4 times as many mangoes as packet B. How many mangoes were there in packet B?

Answer: ☐

45. Mingwei saw the following items on sale.

notebooks
3 for $1

pencils
$2 per bundle

writing pads
$1.20 each

sharpeners
20¢ each

He bought 12 notebooks, 2 bundles of pencils, 4 A4 writing pads and 5 sharpeners.

(a) How much did he spend altogether?

(b) If he gave the cashier a fifty-dollar note, how much change would he receive?

Answer: (a) [   ]

(b) [   ]

Exercise 1

1. (a) 535 **(b)** 723 **(c)** 5 706 **(d)** 7 052 **(e)** 2 088

2. (a) 605 **(b)** 912 **(c)** 2 540 **(d)** 3 005 **(e)** 4 301

3. (a) Four hundred and seven.
(b) Six hundred and forty.
(c) One thousand, seven hundred and one.
(d) Three thousand and seventy-four.
(e) Five thousand, one hundred and twelve.

4. (a) 4, 1, 3, 8 **(b)** 3, 0, 7, 6 **(c)** 5, 8, 4, 0
(d) 3, 4, 0, 5 **(e)** 7, 9, 0, 0

5. (a) 506 **(b)** 380 **(c)** 927 **(d)** 3 048 **(e)** 5 906

6.

600 + 600	70 + 700		30 + 700	10 + 90
800 + 20	400 + 800	450 + 650		200 + 80
110 + 900	**900 + 100**	**800 + 200** / **450 + 550**	**700 + 300** / **400 + 600** / **350 + 650**	650 + 400
150 + 750	250 + 650		**150 + 850**	70 + 830
650 + 35	480 + 52	20 + 80		100 + 90

7. (a) 6 **(b)** 600 **(c)** 6 000
(d) 60 **(e)** 600 **(f)** 6

8. (a) 4 **(b)** 6 **(c)** 0
(d) 4 **(e)** 8

9. (a) 237 **(b)** 580, 600
(c) 1 450, 1 600 **(d)** 4 145, 5 145
(e) 5 600, 8 600

10. (a) 419 **(b)** 361 **(c)** 1 000 **(d)** 4 801 **(e)** 7 120

11. (a) 366 **(b)** 1 547 **(c)** 100 **(d)** 3 056 **(e)** 2 068

12. (a) 200 **(b)** 4 **(c)** 6 000 **(d)** 900 **(e)** 2 345
(f) 6 098 **(g)** 3 402 **(h)** 7 004 **(i)** 2 000, 30
(j) 9 000, 90

13. (a) < **(b)** < **(c)** = **(d)** > **(e)** <

Exercise 2

1. (a) 54 **(b)** 42 **(c)** 65 **(d)** 299 **(e)** 134
(f) 185 **(g)** 255 **(h)** 560 **(i)** 618 **(j)** 784

2. (a) 9 798 **(b)** 3 999 **(c)** 8 377 **(d)** 4 000 **(e)** 4 013
(f) 2 007 **(g)** 3 121 **(h)** 4 689 **(i)** 8 823 **(j)** 1 849
(k) 3 103 **(l)** 2 148 **(m)** 3 505 **(n)** 1 750 **(o)** 825

3. (a) 253 **(b)** 114 **(c)** 711 **(d)** 335 **(e)** 245
(f) 532 **(g)** 289 **(h)** 1 870 **(i)** 2 500

4. (a) 140 **(b)** 590 **(c)** 1 079 **(d)** 2 930 **(e)** 1 950
(f) 2 425 **(g)** 200 **(h)** 3 750 **(i)** 900 **(j)** 820
(k) 1 527 **(l)** 3 087

5. 1 469 **6.** 900 **7.** $2 170

8. 885 **9.** 1 460 **10.** 3 780

Revision 1

Section A

1. (4)	**2.** (4)	**3.** (2)	**4.** (2)	**5.** (3)
6. (3)	**7.** (4)	**8.** (1)	**9.** (2)	**10.** (3)
11. (3)	**12.** (2)	**13.** (3)	**14.** (4)	**15.** (2)
16. (3)	**17.** (2)	**18.** (1)	**19.** (1)	**20.** (1)

Section B

21. 2 035	**22.** 45	**23.** 9 304	**24.** 6 400
25. 272	**26.** 768	**27.** 100	**28.** 1 002, 1 022, 1 202, 1 220
29. 4	**30.** 8 000	**31.** 4 285	**32.** 550
33. 899	**34.** >	**35.** 3 500	**36.** $1 000
37. 2 371	**38.** 1 197	**39.** 4 313	**40.** 2 271

Section C

41. 1 229 bulbs **42.** 2 394 red beads **43.** 312 stamps
44. 535 fish **45.** 1 600 seats

Exercise 3

1. (a) 6, 12	(b) 12, 20	(c) 21, 28	(d) 36, 48	(e) 36, 54
2. (a) 3	(b) 8	(c) 50	(d) 0	(e) 4
(f) 40	(g) 10	(h) 0	(i) 9	(j) 4
(k) 2	(l) 27	(m) 6	(n) 7	
3. (a) ×	(b) ÷	(c) ×	(d) ÷	(e) ÷
(f) ×	(g) ÷	(h) ×	(i) ÷	(j) ×

4.

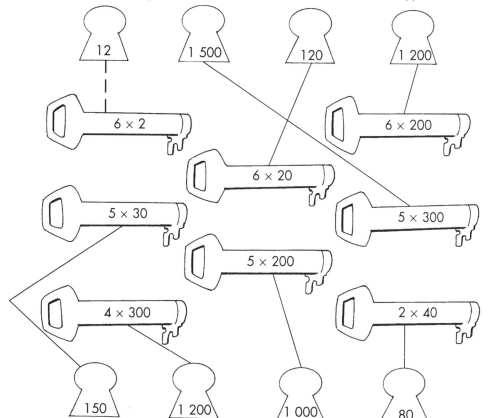

5. (a) 54   (b) 236   (c) 200   (d) 600   (e) 548
   (f) 2 565   (g) 7 000   (h) 744   (i) 2 016   (j) 1 635

6. (a) Quotient: 23, Remainder: 1   (b) Quotient: 21, Remainder: 1
   (c) Quotient: 13, Remainder: 3   (d) Quotient: 36, Remainder: 1
   (e) Quotient: 27, Remainder: 0   (f) Quotient: 23, Remainder: 2

7.

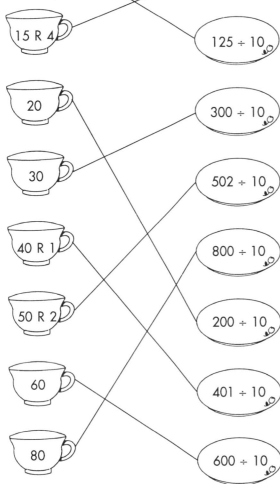

8. 27 stamps

9. 6 chickens

10. 336 chairs

11. $18

12. 16 exercise books

13. 195 cents or $1.95

14. 18 pages

15. $140

Exercise 4

1. (a) **6** × 2 = 12, 12 ÷ 2 = **6**   (b) **7** × 3 = 21, 21 ÷ 3 = **7**
   (c) **8** × 2 = 16, 16 ÷ 2 = **8**   (d) **9** × 4 = 36, 36 ÷ 4 = **9**
   (e) 4 × **6** = 24, 24 ÷ 4 = **6**   (f) 5 × **7** = 35, 35 ÷ 5 = **7**
   (g) 4 × **8** = 32, 32 ÷ 4 = **8**   (h) 6 × **9** = 54, 54 ÷ 6 = **9**
   (i) 8 × **6** = 48, 48 ÷ 8 = **6**   (j) 2 × **9** = 18, 18 ÷ 2 = **9**

2. (a) 96   (b) 119   (c) 168   (d) 108   (e) 270
   (f) 558   (g) 224   (h) 432   (i) 702   (j) 720
   (k) 1 484   (l) 2 624   (m) 3 726   (n) 984   (o) 3 006
   (p) 4 291   (q) 5 768   (r) 5 406

3. (a) 14   (b) 12   (c) 6   (d) 12   (e) 18
   (f) 18   (g) 14   (h) 20   (i) 13   (j) 17
   (k) 61   (l) 24   (m) 8   (n) 9   (o) 7
   (p) 6   (q) 8   (r) 9

4. (a) Quotient: 14, Remainder: 6   (b) Quotient: 33, Remainder: 3
   (c) Quotient: 39, Remainder: 6   (d) Quotient: 89, Remainder: 2

(e) Quotient: 63, Remainder: 1   (f) Quotient: 74, Remainder: 2
(g) Quotient: 71, Remainder: 2   (h) Quotient: 92, Remainder: 5
(i) Quotient: 93, Remainder: 5   (j) Quotient: 103, Remainder: 1

5. 14 children   6. 720 fruits   7. 145 letters
8. 65 sweets   9. 75 rambutans   10. 136 baskets of durians
11. (a) 39 bags   (b) 2 oranges   12. 1 410 people

Revision 2

Section A

1. (4)   2. (2)   3. (2)   4. (4)   5. (4)
6. (1)   7. (3)   8. (1)   9. (2)   10. (2)
11. (4)   12. (2)   13. (4)   14. (4)   15. (3)
16. (1)   17. (4)   18. (4)   19. (3)   20. (2)

Section B

21. 3 047   22. 4 470   23. 1   24. 10   25. 3 099
26. 0   27. +   28. 5 608   29. 40   30. 500
31. 6   32. 6 600   33. 125   34. 130   35. $<$
36. 45   37. 10   38. 48   39. 45   40. 598

Section C

41. 763 leaves   42. 714 empty lots   43. 60 boxes
44. 1 650 carnations and orchids   45. 1 870 guppies and goldfish

Continual Assessment 1

Section A

1. (3)   2. (1)   3. (3)   4. (1)   5. (3)
6. (2)   7. (3)   8. (4)   9. (4)   10. (3)
11. (2)   12. (3)   13. (2)   14. (3)   15. (2)
16. (4)   17. (2)   18. (2)   19. (1)   20. (3)

Section B

21. 8 317   22. 104   23. 8 421
24. 530, 503, 350, 305   25. $>$ 26. 1 000
27. 10   28. 1 944   29. 1 259
30. 2   31. 8   32. 8
33. 9 000   34. 3   35. $=$
36. $<$ 37. 905   38. 2 091
39. 255   40. 6

Section C

41. 595 oranges   42. $1 760   43. 4 613 children
44. 175 sweets   45. 1 172 marbles

Exercise 5

1. (a) 5 (b) 7 (c) 6 (d) 4
   (e) CD (f) GH (g) 3 cm
2. (a) 150 cm (b) Ahmad (c) Amin (d) 24 cm
3. (a) 58 (b) 63 (c) 72 (d) 45
   (e) 65 (f) 37 (g) 38 (h) 45
4. (a) > (b) < (c) = (d) >
5. (a) 110 (b) 1, 0 (c) 200 (d) 2, 0
   (e) 205 (f) 1, 85 (g) 365 (h) 2, 35
6. (a) 1, 85 (b) 3, 10 (c) 5, 25 (d) 4, 0 (e) 1, 50
7. (a) 0, 75 (b) 1, 50 (c) 1, 75 (d) 1, 50 (e) 1, 25
8. (a) 1 500 (b) 2 200 m (c) 1, 750 (d) 2, 50 (e) 2, 0
   (f) 4, 0 (g) 550 (h) 0, 500 (i) 0, 630 (j) 1 500
9. (a) 1 m 59 cm or 159 cm (b) 17 cm (c) 4 m 55 cm or 455 cm
10. (a) $25\frac{1}{2}$ (b) 12 (c) via C
11. (a) Eugene (b) 2 m 99 cm (c) Ashok
12. (a) 540 m (b) 800 m (c) Eugene, 260 m
13. (a) 10 m 50 cm (b) 50 cm (c) 2 m
14. (a) the pond (b) 58 m 15. 850 cm 16. 91 cm
17. (a) Malacca (b) 81 km
18. (a) 13, 450 (b) 7, 0 (c) 1, 250 (d) 9, 800 (e) 8, 250

Exercise 6

1. (a) 2, 700 (b) 1, 300 (c) 0, 900 (d) 3, 400 (e) 1, 800
   (f) 2, 800
2. (a) 700 (b) 300 (c) 766 (d) 750 (e) 360
   (f) 656 (g) 1 000 (h) 1 800 (i) 6, 600 (j) 3, 600
3. (a) 1 300 (b) 2, 800 (c) 2 450 (d) 3, 70 (e) 1 265
   (f) 3, 826 (g) 2 805 (h) 1, 400 (i) 3 060 (j) 4, 5
4. (a) 340 (b) 190
5. (a) 290 (b) 180
6. (a) 380 (b) 90 (c) 45
7. (a) 390 (b) 200 (c) 40
8. (a) coffee powder (b) tea bags (c) 1 000 (d) 990 (e) 580
   (f) 330 (g) 1, 500 (h) 2
9. (a) 1 068, 1, 68 (b) 1 000, 1, 0 (c) 1 602, 1, 602
   (d) 3, 804, 3 804 (e) 6, 958, 6 958 (f) 8, 710, 8 710
   (g) 1 110, 1, 110 (h) 2 280, 2, 280 (i) 1 272, 1, 272
   (j) 1 548, 1, 548 (k) 2 472, 2, 472 (l) 5 048, 5, 48
   (m) 837 g (n) 530 g
10. 4, 640 11. 510 packets 12. 7 500
13. 600 14. 19 15. 127, 900
16. 20, 0 17. 20 18. 23, 0
19. 1, 50

First Semestral Examination

Section A

1. (3)	**2.** (1)	**3.** (2)	**4.** (3)	**5.** (3)
6. (4)	**7.** (4)	**8.** (2)	**9.** (2)	**10.** (4)
11. (3)	**12.** (3)	**13.** (1)	**14.** (3)	**15.** (4)
16. (1)	**17.** (4)	**18.** (2)	**19.** (2)	**20.** (2)

Section B

21. 1 028	**22.** 18	**23.** 4 608	**24.** 72	**25.** 90
26. 155	**27.** 500	**28.** 3 000	**29.** 100	**30.** 6 532
31. 103	**32.** 4	**33.** 30	**34.** 88	**35.** 1, 50
36. 3, 400	**37.** 900	**38.** 1, 800	**39.** 6 915	**40.** 18

Section C

41. 1 258 rubber bands   **42.** 400 m   **43.** 2 842 pencils

44. 81 trays   **45.** $16

Exercise 7

1. 450, 870
   (a) 420 + 30 = 450, 450
   (b) 420 + 450 = 870, 870
   (c) 870 − 48 = 822, 822
2. $50, $75
   (a) $25 + $50 = $75, $75
   (b) $75 − $25 = $50, $50
3. 24, 8
   (a) 32 ÷ 4 = 8, 8
   (b) 8 × 3 = 24, 24
4. $100 − $12 = $88, 4 units = $88, 1 unit = $22, $22
5. 86 + 75 = 161, 500 − 161 = 339, 339
6. 28 + 1 756 = 1 784, 2 855 − 1 784 = 1 071, 1 071
7. $1 300 − $352 = $948, $948 ÷ 6 = $158, $158
8. 200, 200, 50 × 4 = 200, 40 + 200 = 240, 240
9. 17 girls   10. 120 marbles
11. 35 beads   12. 17 sandwiches
13. (a) 8 trays   (b) 2 eggs

Exercise 8

1. (a) 92   (b) 166   (c) 306
   (d) 56, 52, 52   (e) 146, 143, 143   (f) 160, 152, 152
   (g) 800, 790, 786, 786   (h) 200, 243, 243   (i) 400, 482, 482
   (j) 500, 564, 564   (k) 840, 836, 836   (l) 720, 711, 711
   (m) 600, 591, 591   (n) 900, 870, 870   (o) 700, 725, 725
   (p) 500, 513, 513

2.

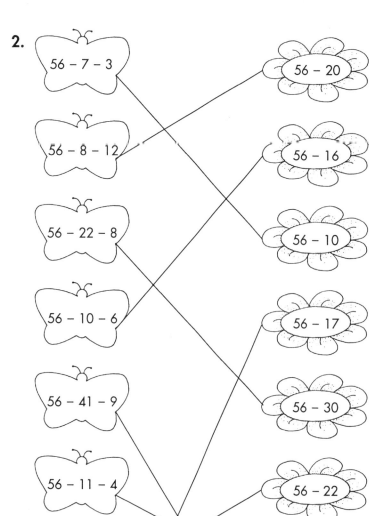

3. (a) 10, 60
(b) 20, 120
(c) 30, 208
(d) 200, 1, 341
(e) 300, 1, 168
(f) 99, 1, 208
(g) 200, 2, 302
(h) 156, 200 + 78, 278
(i) 200, 403 + 35, 438
(j) 700, 217 + 26, 243

Exercise 9

1. (a) $0.65   (b) $1.00   (c) $1.25   (d) $6.55
(e) $25.15   (f) $16.30

2.

	$10	$5	$1	50¢	20¢	10¢	5¢
$3.60			3	1		1	
$4.55			4	1			1
$5.90		1		1	2		
$6.15		1	1			1	1
$7.35		1	2		1	1	1
$8.75		1	3	1	1		1
$5.25		1				1	1
$12.10	1		2			1	
$13.70	1		3	1	1		
$25.20	2	1			1		
$32.65	3		2	1		1	1
$26.50	2	1	1	1			

3. (a) 0.85   (b) 2.08
(c) 12.40

4. (a) forty-five cents
(b) five dollars and eighty cents
(c) ten dollars and six cents
(d) three hundred and eighty-six dollars
(e) one thousand, five hundred and eighty-eight dollars
(f) six thousand, five hundred and fourteen dollars

5. (a) 1.25   (b) 25   (c) 3.40
(d) 670   (e) 16.70   (f) 1 105
(g) 39.05   (h) 2 280

192

6. (a) 1 413, 1 413.08   (b) 90.90, 91.50   (c) 121.20, 121.35
   (d) 185.02, 185.37   (e) 50.20   (f) 305.09
   (g) 2 058

7. (a) 105, 1.05   (b) 160, 1.60   (c) 170, 1.70
   (d) 150, 1.50

8. (a) $5.90   (b) $7.90   (c) $10.40
   (d) $28.30   (e) $50.00   (f) $100.00

9. (a) 5.20, 5.14   (b) 3.50, 3.46   (c) 31, 30.70
   (d) 66.40, 65.55

10. (a) $33.55   (b) $21.20   (c) $70.92
   (d) $26.47   (e) $4.84   (f) $12.36

11. (a) $1.50   (b) $3.24   (c) $50.60   (d) $38.00   (e) $3.85
   (f) $27.60   (g) $14.88   (h) $54.60   (i) $44.10

12. (a) $2.00   (b) $3.09   (c) $0.30   (d) $1.76   (e) $0.43
   (f) $0.70   (g) $1.09   (h) $0.67   (i) $0.13

13. (a) 3.90, 29.00, $32.90, $17.10
   (b) 18.90, 4.50, 23.40, 6.60
   (c) 5.10, 7.80, 4.50, 17.40, 2.60
   (d) 37.80, 25.80, 29.00, 92.60, 7.40

14. $15.50   15. $31.60   16. $47.50

17. $8.90   18. $9.50   19. $3.55

20. $3.95   21. $76.50   22. $9.30

23. $35.50   24. (a) $1.20   (b) $0.80

25. $7.00

Revision 3

Section A

1. (2)   2. (1)   3. (3)   4. (3)   5. (3)
6. (4)   7. (4)   8. (4)   9. (4)   10. (1)
11. (2)   12. (4)   13. (3)   14. (2)   15. (2)
16. (2)   17. (4)   18. (1)   19. (3)   20. (2)

Section B

21. 6 301   22. 20   23. =   24. 164   25. 184
26. 67   27. 56   28. 1 500   29. 36   30. 3, 550
31. 410   32. 165   33. 3.25   34. 0.80   35. 0.90
36. 2   37. 8   38. $1.50   39. 40   40. 190

Section C

41. $15   42. $35.75   43. 72 kg   44. $41.60   45. $10.50

Exercise 10

1. (a) 700   (b) 300   (c) 400   (d) 250   (e) 150   (f) 750
2. (a) 440   (b) 680   (c) 550   (d) 750   (e) 700

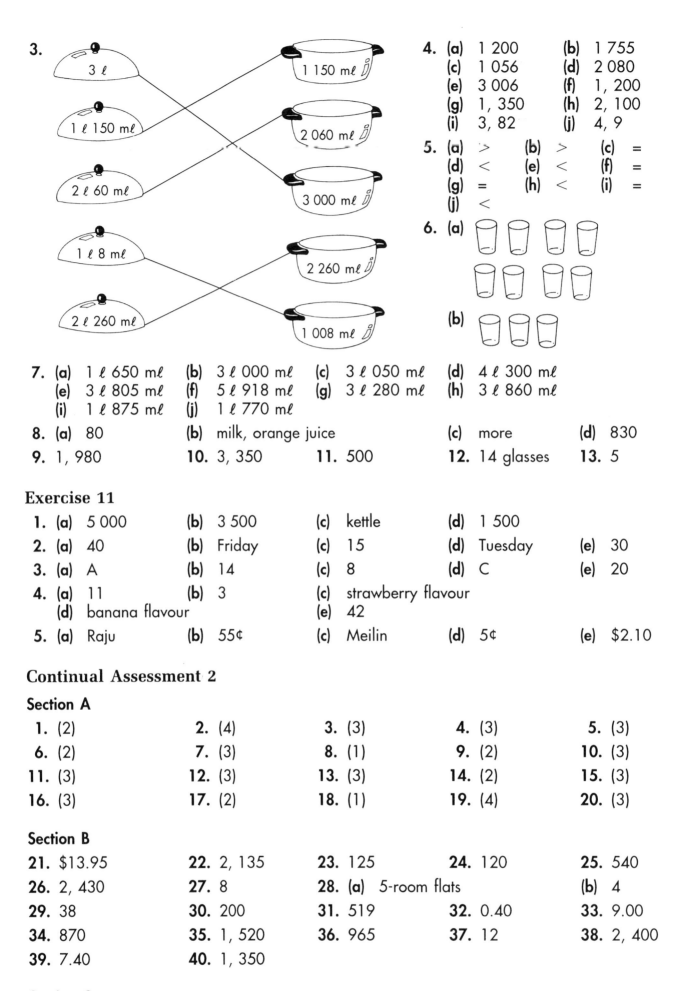

3.

(3 ℓ → 2 060 mℓ)
(1 ℓ 150 mℓ → 1 150 mℓ)
(2 ℓ 60 mℓ → 3 000 mℓ)
(1 ℓ 8 mℓ → 1 008 mℓ)
(2 ℓ 260 mℓ → 2 260 mℓ)

4. (a) 1 200   (b) 1 755
     (c) 1 056   (d) 2 080
     (e) 3 006   (f) 1, 200
     (g) 1, 350   (h) 2, 100
     (i) 3, 82   (j) 4, 9

5. (a) >   (b) >   (c) =
     (d) <   (e) <   (f) =
     (g) =   (h) <   (i) =
     (j) <

6. (a)

(b)

7. (a) 1 ℓ 650 mℓ   (b) 3 ℓ 000 mℓ   (c) 3 ℓ 050 mℓ   (d) 4 ℓ 300 mℓ
     (e) 3 ℓ 805 mℓ   (f) 5 ℓ 918 mℓ   (g) 3 ℓ 280 mℓ   (h) 3 ℓ 860 mℓ
     (i) 1 ℓ 875 mℓ   (j) 1 ℓ 770 mℓ

8. (a) 80   (b) milk, orange juice   (c) more   (d) 830

9. 1, 980   **10.** 3, 350   **11.** 500   **12.** 14 glasses   **13.** 5

Exercise 11

1. (a) 5 000   (b) 3 500   (c) kettle   (d) 1 500

2. (a) 40   (b) Friday   (c) 15   (d) Tuesday   (e) 30

3. (a) A   (b) 14   (c) 8   (d) C   (e) 20

4. (a) 11   (b) 3   (c) strawberry flavour
     (d) banana flavour   (e) 42

5. (a) Raju   (b) 55¢   (c) Meilin   (d) 5¢   (e) $2.10

Continual Assessment 2

Section A

1. (2)   **2.** (4)   **3.** (3)   **4.** (3)   **5.** (3)
6. (2)   **7.** (3)   **8.** (1)   **9.** (2)   **10.** (3)
11. (3)   **12.** (3)   **13.** (3)   **14.** (2)   **15.** (3)
16. (3)   **17.** (2)   **18.** (1)   **19.** (4)   **20.** (3)

Section B

21. $13.95   **22.** 2, 135   **23.** 125   **24.** 120   **25.** 540
26. 2, 430   **27.** 8   **28.** (a) 5-room flats   (b) 4
29. 38   **30.** 200   **31.** 519   **32.** 0.40   **33.** 9.00
34. 870   **35.** 1, 520   **36.** 965   **37.** 12   **38.** 2, 400
39. 7.40   **40.** 1, 350

Section C

41. 1 334 stamps   **42.** $7   **43.** 8 598 concert tickets
44. $8.60   **45.** $48

Exercise 12

1. (a)  (b)

2. (a) $\frac{3}{6}$ or $\frac{1}{2}$ (b) $\frac{2}{3}$ 3. (a) C (b) B

4. (a) $\frac{5}{8}$ (b) $\frac{3}{5}$ (c) $\frac{1}{6}$ (d) $\frac{5}{8}$

   (e) $\frac{5}{8}$ (f) $\frac{1}{4}$ (g) $\frac{3}{4}$ (h) $\frac{6}{8}$

5. (a) (b) (c)

   (d) (e) (f)

6. (a) 5, 8 (b) 8, 5 (c) $\frac{3}{8}$

7. (a) 7 (b) 9

8. (a) $\frac{1}{7}$ (b) $\frac{1}{5}$ (c) $\frac{2}{6}$ (d) $\frac{8}{9}$

9. (a) $\frac{1}{8}$ (b) $\frac{1}{10}$ (c) $\frac{7}{14}$ (d) $\frac{4}{16}$

10. (a) $\frac{1}{10}, \frac{1}{6}, \frac{1}{4}$ (b) $\frac{2}{9}, \frac{2}{7}, \frac{2}{3}$

11. (a) $\frac{1}{5}, \frac{1}{6}, \frac{1}{8}$ (b) $\frac{4}{9}, \frac{4}{12}, \frac{4}{14}$

12. (a) $\frac{5}{9}, \frac{6}{9}, \frac{7}{9}, \frac{8}{9}, \frac{9}{9}$ (b) $\frac{4}{6}, \frac{3}{6}, \frac{2}{6}, \frac{1}{6}$

13. (a) > (b) <

14. (a) 2 (b) 3 (c) 10 (d) 5 (e) 9, 4 (f) 4, 2

15. (a) $\frac{6}{16}$ (b) $\frac{4}{8}$ (c) $\frac{14}{24}$ (d) $\frac{5}{8}$

16. (a) < (b) > (c) < (d) >

17. (a) $\frac{1}{2}, \frac{3}{5}, \frac{4}{6}$ (b) $\frac{1}{8}, \frac{2}{10}, \frac{1}{3}$

18. (a) $\frac{4}{4}$ or 1 (b) $\frac{7}{10}$ (c) $1\frac{1}{2}$ (d) $\frac{4}{5}$ (e) $\frac{12}{12}$ or 1

    (f) $\frac{14}{10}$ or $1\frac{4}{10}$ (g) $\frac{7}{8}$ (h) $\frac{7}{6}$ or $1\frac{1}{6}$ (i) $\frac{10}{10}$ or 1 (j) $\frac{6}{6}$ or 1

19. (a) 0 (b) $\frac{2}{8}$ (c) $\frac{3}{10}$ (d) $\frac{2}{9}$ (e) $\frac{3}{8}$

    (f) $\frac{1}{12}$ (g) $\frac{3}{6}$ (h) $\frac{3}{6}$ (i) $\frac{1}{6}$ (j) $\frac{8}{12}$

20. $\frac{2}{3}$ 21. $\frac{1}{4}$ 22. 9   23. $5   24. $\frac{1}{4}$ m

Exercise 13

1.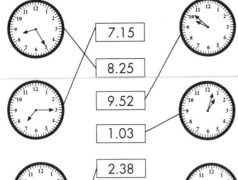

2. (a) 9.35   (b) 10 o'clock or 10.00
(c) 3.22   (d) 12.05
(e) 2.34   (f) 6.43

3. (a) (b) (c)
(d) (e) (f)

4. (a) 45   (b) 2   (c) 3, 35

5. (a) 80   (b) 1, 40   (c) 120
(d) 1, 0   (e) 90   (f) 2, 20
(g) 160   (h) 3, 20   (i) 190
(j) 1, 26   (k) 205   (l) 2, 15

6. (a) 60 min = 1 h 0 min   (b) 87 min = 1 h 27 min   (c) 77 min = 1 h 17 min
(d) 63 min = 1 h 3 min   (e) 90 min = 1 h 30 min   (f) 80 min = 1 h 20 min

7. (a) 66 min = 1 h 6 min   (b) 67 min = 1 h 7 min   (c) 70 min = 1 h 10 min
(d) 64 min = 1 h 4 min   (e) 76 min = 1 h 16 min   (f) 62 min = 1 h 2 min

8. (a) 50   (b) 32   (c) 42
(d) 36   (e) 180   (f) 3, 45

9.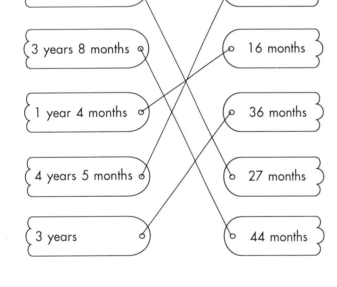

10. (a) 2, 4   (b) 3, 11
(c) 1, 6   (d) 4, 2

11. (a) 25   (b) 13
(c) 37   (d) 33

12. (a) 2, 1   (b) 4, 1
(c) 5, 3   (d) 9, 1

13. 75   14. 5
15. 1, 25   16. 47

Revision 4

Section A

1. (3)   2. (4)   3. (2)   4. (4)   5. (3)
6. (3)   7. (1)   8. (2)   9. (3)   10. (3)
11. (2)   12. (2)   13. (2)   14. (3)   15. (1)
16. (2)   17. (3)   18. (1)   19. (1)   20. (3)

Section B

21. 2 100 **22.** 6.15 **23.** 90 **24.** 44, 500 **25.** 45

26. 1 575 **27.** **28.** $\frac{1}{12}$ **29.** 4 023 **30.** 26

31. 1, 35 **32.** 2.20 **33.** 6, 750 **34.** 6 **35.** 1.10

36. 147 **37.** 6, 20 **38.** $\frac{1}{7}$ **39.** 42 **40.** 7

Section C

41. 784 girls **42.** 3 500 **43.** $\frac{2}{15}$ **44.** 6.40 a.m. **45.** 17.50

Exercise 14

1.

Figure	Number of sides	Number of angles
A	4	4
B	3	3
C	5	5
D	6	6
E	7	7
F	8	8

2.

Smaller than a right angle	Equal to a right angle	Bigger than a right angle
a	b	c
f	d	e
	h	g

3. (a) 5, 2 (b) 4, 4 (c) 6, 1 (d) 6, 3 (e) 7, 0
(f) 12, 4 (g) 7, 3

Exercise 15

1. (a)  (b)  **2.** (a) (b)

3. (a) 18 (b) 12 cm (c) B (d) A

4. (a) 12 (b) 12 (c) 9 (d) 10
(e) 11 (f) 8 (g) 9 (h) 13

5. (a) 27 (b) 33 (c) 39 (d) 18
(e) 36 (f) 28 (g) 24 (h) 40

6. (a) B   (b) B   (c) D   7. (a) B   (b) 12   (c) C

8. (a) 29   (b) 40   (c) 28   9. (a) 48   (b) 150   (c) 160

Final Semestral Examination

Section A

1. (3)	**2.** (2)	**3.** (1)	**4.** (4)	**5.** (2)
6. (1)	**7.** (4)	**8.** (3)	**9.** (1)	**10.** (3)
11. (1)	**12.** (4)	**13.** (4)	**14.** (2)	**15.** (4)
16. (4)	**17.** (3)	**18.** (4)	**19.** (2)	**20.** (3)

Section B

21. 660	**22.** 2	**23.** 2 856	**24.** 5	**25.** 120
26. 378	**27.** $2.25	**28.** 12	**29.** 28	**30.** $\frac{2}{12}$ or $\frac{1}{6}$
31. $\frac{5}{8}$	**32.** 1, 20	**33.** 4, 10	**34.** 11	**35.** 81
36. 5	**37.** 24	**38.** Friday	**39.** 20	**40.** 300

Section C

41. 2 386 stamps   **42.** $\frac{4}{15}$ **43.** 2 kg 537 g

44. 24 mangoes   **45.** (a) $13.80   (b) $36.20